THE SALESMAN
IN THE FIELD

Conditions of work and employment
of commercial travellers and representatives

Michael Bell

International Labour Office   Geneva

ISBN 92-2-102308-7

First published 1980

Printed by the International Labour Office, Geneva, Switzerland

CONTENTS

INTRODUCTION

The problems of commercial travellers were formally considered for the first time within the ILO before the Second World War, in the context of the work of the Advisory Committee on Salaried Employees which, at its Third Session (Geneva, 3-4 April 1935), discussed "the legal position of commercial and industrial travellers and representatives".

The Advisory Committee formulated a resolution on problems of the profession which it deemed to be of particular urgency, and in particular those arising from the absence, in many countries, of any legal definition of the terms "traveller" and "representative" and the ensuing uncertainty regarding their entitlement to the protection and benefits of social and labour legislation.

In that resolution the Advisory Committee expressed the wish that -

"(a) in every country regulations should be issued to define the legal status of travellers and representatives, which, while taking into account their special conditions of employment, should place them under the legislation for the social protection, insurance and welfare of salaried employees;

(b) the said regulations should cover all travellers and representatives, even if they work for several firms or are paid solely on commission, provided that they do not engage in transactions on their own account and that the contracts binding them to the firm or firms that they represent state the nature of the article for sale, the area within which they are to carry on their activities, and the rate of their remuneration or commission;

(c) the regulations should provide among other things for -
(i) compulsory written contracts; (ii) a period of notice of not less than three months for termination of the contract; (iii) the complete freedom of the traveller or representative from financial liability in the event of the insolvency of the buyer; (iv) recognition of the right to special compensation representing the traveller's or representative's personal share in the growth of the number and value of the circle of customers obtained for the firm through his activities."

In the same resolution the Advisory Committee also suggested that the conditions of employment of travellers and representatives should be fixed by collective agreement within the limits prescribed by legislation.

Since the Second World War, the Advisory Committee on Salaried Employees and Professional Workers, set up in 1947, has on a number of occasions requested the Office to undertake studies of the conditions of work and employment of commercial travellers, agents and similar categories of non-manual workers.

Under the ILO's programme of work for 1978-79, a study was to have been carried out on the employment conditions and conditions of work of commercial travellers and insurance representatives. However, in the course of the information-gathering activities which preceded the actual writing, it became clear that there were

fundamental differences in the structure of the two professions and
the nature of the work performed by them. In particular, the
element of direct, individual initiative in seeking out custom,
which is a fundamental feature of the work of commercial travellers
and representatives, is not a consistently apparent feature of that
of insurance representatives in all countries; moreover, the profession of commercial traveller or representative cuts horizontally
across large areas of commerce and industry, whereas that of insurance representative is integrated vertically into a single, homo-
geneous sector of the economy. It was therefore decided to
examine the conditions of work and employment of the two groups
separately.

A substantial body of information was provided by 31 governments[1] in reply to a questionnaire sent out by the ILO at the end
of 1978. In addition, several organisations affiliated to the
International Federation of Commercial, Clerical and Technical
Employees (FIET) provided information on matters raised in the
questionnaire. While this coverage is not as complete as might
have been wished, the fact that the profession appears to be con-
centrated in a relatively small number of countries which have
achieved a certain minimum level of industrial development may make
some of the gaps less important than they would otherwise have been.

The study, which was written by Mr. Michael Bell of the
Salaried Employees and Professional Workers Branch, seeks to des-
cribe the conditions of work and employment of commercial travellers
today, in particular as they are affected by the special nature of
their relationships with their principals and the special conditions
under which their work is performed. It bears in mind in particular the problems to which the 1935 meeting drew attention and the
progress made towards their solution.

Since in many countries commercial travellers working under de
facto employment relationships now enjoy employee status, its primary purpose is to examine their situation and problems within this
new status. However, since their actual duties and functions continue to be similar to those of commercial agents with self-employed
status, and in view of the close links which exist between the two
groups in a number of countries, it is difficult to separate the two
completely. Consequently, comparisons with the situation of commercial agents, and references to advances in the social field won by
them, will be found in various parts of the text.

The study examines successively the function and characteristics
of the profession, with special reference to developments on the
question of the circumstances in which commercial representatives
enjoy employee status; preparation for the profession and career
development; the obligations of employees in general as applicable
to commercial travellers and representatives, and special aspects of
their conditions of work and employment; remuneration and expenses;
social protection; termination, with special reference to goodwill
indemnities and the application of the radius clause; and the
problems of certain special categories of external salesmen.
Finally, it attempts to sum up the situation regarding the questions

---

[1] Argentina, Australia, Austria, Belgium, Chile, Colombia,
Denmark, Ecuador, Egypt, Ethiopia, Finland, France, Germany (Federal
Republic), Hungary, Ireland, Italy, Malaysia, Mexico, Netherlands,
New Zealand, Norway, Panama, Peru, Pakistan, Philippines, Poland,
Spain, Sweden, Switzerland, United Kingdom, Uruguay.

raised at the 1935 meeting and to identify certain problems which appear to have acquired prominence as a result of the conferment of employee status on commercial travellers and representatives.

The study does not claim to be a comprehensive review of the position of commercial travellers in all countries. In several countries the profession is not treated as a separate entity for purposes of setting conditions of employment; in others separate statistics on the profession, or inquiries into their specific problems, are not available. It seeks, on the basis of examples encountered in individual countries, to draw attention to what appear to be the main problems relating to the conditions of work and employment of commercial travellers and, where applicable, the ways in which they have been dealt with.

＊

＊　　　　＊

TERMINOLOGY: A PRELIMINARY NOTE

A problem arises regarding the choice of the terms to be used to designate the different types of commercial travellers.

The most recent (1968) edition of the International Standard Classification of Occupations (ISCO) gives the following definition of commercial travellers:

"**4.32 Commercial travellers and manufacturers' agents**

Workers in this unit group sell goods on a wholesale basis in an allotted geographical area. Their functions include:

soliciting orders and selling goods to retail, industrial, wholesale and other establishments;

selling products of one or more home or foreign manufacturers to wholesale, retail and other establishments.

4.32.20 Commercial traveller -

solicits orders by personally visiting clients and sells goods to retailers, industrial consumers, institutional and professional establishments or wholesale organisations in an allotted geographical area;

attempts to interest prospective buyers by showing sample articles or indicating products in catalogue and pointing out merits; quotes prices, credit terms and delivery conditions, offers reductions in certain circumstances and gives information concerning probable price trends; forwards orders to office and makes reports of business transactions; studies trade periodicals and keeps himself informed of price changes and other marketing conditions."

ISCO also distinguishes a separate category - the manufacturers' agent - who "sells products of one or more home or foreign manufacturers on a commission basis, in an allotted geographical area" but who "performs essentially the same duties as described under Commercial traveller".

As a result of recent developments in the profession, this method of classification no longer fully reflects reality in all countries where commercial travellers are found in significant numbers. In particular, the concept of the commercial traveller is today in practice frequently extended to embrace certain members of other occupational categories in other unit groups of ISCO. Thus, for instance, a technical salesman (category 4.31.20), who

"calls on architects, engineers and other potential users to explain merits of his firm's product and its application to the user's special requirements, prepares or arranges for the preparation of plans and operational specifications showing gains from proposed changes in equipment, methods or materials. May negotiate contracts and assist in the arrangement of credit"

is performing functions similar to those of a commercial traveller as defined, the only difference being that the products offered by the technical salesman, and the arrangements for the sales, are more complex. The functions of a "business services salesman" (except advertising, which is covered in category 4.42.20), who -

"interviews prospective clients and explains features and benefits of service; quotes prices and credit terms; prepares contract forms"

might equally be considered to be similar to that of a commercial traveller, to the extent that he goes out to seek or visit customers.

The feature common to all is that they are external salesmen, i.e. they look for and deal with customers or prospects away from the offices of the firms employing them.

In addition, it is necessary, for the purposes of this study, to distinguish two types of commercial travellers: those working for a single employer and those working for more than one employer, since the position and the problems of the two groups differ in a number of respects. It is difficult to make this distinction on the basis of the ISCO terminology and definitions.

Thus, the choice of terminology, in a study covering a number of countries, is not easy if misunderstandings are to be avoided.

For instance, the word "representative" denotes in current usage in the United Kingdom an external salesman employed by a single firm; the French word "représentant" refers to an external salesman working as an employee for more than one firm; while the German and Italian equivalents (respectively "Handelsvertreter" and "rappresentante") refer to persons performing the same type of work but with self-employed status. Additional problems arise from differences of usage in countries with the same official language; thus the term used to designate a commercial traveller in Argentine legislation ("viajante de comercio") is considered ambiguous in Spain, where, however, the term "agente commercial" (which in most other countries denotes an external salesman with self-employed status) is used to designate certain categories of external salesmen in employment relationships as well as those who are self-employed. Thus, any choice of terms must inevitably be to some extent arbitrary.

As far as the English language is concerned, the term "commercial traveller" is less frequently heard now than at the time of the 1935 meeting of the Advisory Committee on Salaried Employees. Other terms have gained currency; thus in the United Kingdom a commercial traveller working for one employer may be designated "sales representative" (the title most frequently used), "sales executive", "sales engineer", "sales professional", "salesman", "sales agent" and even "agent". However, the term "commercial traveller" is still in widespread use and has the merit of maintaining continuity with earlier work done in the ILO on the subject.

Consequently, for purposes of clarity, the term "commercial traveller"[1] will be used in this study to designate a worker who habitually goes out to customers and prospects to solicit orders on

---

[1] In French: voyageur de commerce; in Spanish (Argentina): viajante de comercio.

behalf of a single firm, and who has the status of an employee of that firm.   A worker performing the same functions, also with employee status, but for more than one employer (or for one employer but with the freedom to work for more than one if he so desires), will be designated by the term "representative".[1]   The term "commercial agent" refers to a person performing similar functions, but in a non-employment relationship with one or more principals.   The term "external salesman" or "salesman" is used when no specific category is referred to.

---

[1] In French: représentant;   in Spanish (Argentina): representante (de comercio).

CHAPTER I

FUNCTION AND CHARACTERISTICS OF THE PROFESSION

Origins and nature of the profession

The function of the commercial traveller or representative as we know it today is of relatively recent origin.

Until the time of the Industrial Revolution economies were relatively self-sufficient in character, with most production being designed to satisfy local needs and sold in local markets. A relatively small, but continually expanding, range of goods was traded on an inter-city or an international basis; but trading methods were for understandable reasons based primarily on the direct physical transfer of goods, against cash payment (or possibly bankers' draft), after due examination, from seller to buyer at each stage in the process of transfer from producer to consumer. Thus, a merchant had to transport with him all the goods he planned to sell during a particular journey - although he might entrust the actual conduct of the journey to an agent or make arrangements with an agent in another town to sell the goods for him against a fee or commission. There was also the class of itinerant vendors, hawking their wares from village to village. These categories of salesmen still exist today.

However, with the coming of the Industrial Revolution, and the accompanying improvements in transport and communications and in banking and audit facilities, came radical changes in patterns of trading. The potential economies of large-scale production offered vast new opportunities for selling and made it necessary to seek out those opportunities, to be continually in search of new customers. In such circumstances travelling with one's entire stock-in-trade was hardly feasible. However, the fact that in a system of mechanised production every item in a given line of goods is normally an exact copy of every other item made it possible to sell by demonstrating samples. Thus, a prospective customer could be shown a sample which he could inspect and, if necessary test, and on the basis of that inspection place an order for a large number of similar items which might not yet have been manufactured but which he could be reasonably sure would satisfy his requirements in the same way as the sample itself. Thus, a salesman representing the producing firm, armed with samples of the firm's product, could bring the latter to the attention of a large number of potential customers - whether buying for sale to others or for their own production requirements - who might not, without the salesman's visit, have learnt of the product's existence, and give them an opportunity of examining and discussing it without having to go out of their way to do so. If the product was suitable, the salesman would take orders for future delivery, which the producing firm could either meet from stock or make provision for in its production plans. Even if the salesman did not succeed in obtaining an order, he frequently picked up valuable information on the state of the market, sometimes from the very reasons for refusal - the price was too high, the standard of quality was not in line with the customer's needs, a competing product was more suitable, or customer preferences were currently directed towards other types of product. This information could be valuable to the producer.

The advantages of this method of selling were soon appreciated by both buyers and sellers, and the profession of external salesman expanded rapidly.

A further development which began at about this time affected the status of the profession. While agents have been known at least since the Middle Ages, they were usually independent traders in their own right, operating for their own account and concentrating their attention on the merchandise they considered was most likely to find a ready sale. As production expanded and competition intensified, it became of increasing interest to manufacturers to seek out persons who would act on their behalf to promote sales of their products under a formal contract of representation, under which the salesman would undertake to devote himself to promoting sales of the goods of the manufacturer concerned. He might give this undertaking on an exclusive basis, agreeing to devote himself full time to the task; alternatively, he might wish to conserve the right to sell other lines of goods, undertaking only not to sell any goods competing with those of the principal. Initially, two categories of salesmen developed, both performing substantially the same functions: the independent commercial agent and the commercial traveller or sales representative with employee status. As will be seen later, for many years, in view of the uncertainty of existing legislation on the subject, the distinction between the two categories and the line of demarcation separating them have been unclear; this problem was one of the principal subjects of concern to commercial travellers during the inter-war period. Since then, however, as labour legislation in particular has developed, substantial progress has been made towards the solution of at least the legal aspects of the question in the different countries, although the actual functions of the two categories remain extremely similar.

Today, in most market economies at least, the external salesman is recognised to be an essential link in the machinery of production and commerce. He brings new products to established and potential customers, and by a combination of direct demonstration together with comment, explanation and personal persuasion, he seeks to obtain outlets for the goods (or services) provided by the firm he represents. His own personality can in fact be as important as the quality and the suitability of the goods he has to offer; for to the potential buyer he may set the image of the firm as a whole. At the same time, he keeps his principal informed on the state of the market. In recent years, as the range, variety and complexity of the products available on the market have increased, and in the face of ever-increasing competition, he has had to take on new functions, sometimes calling for technical as well as commercial expertise; many external salesmen are frequently called upon to advise their customers on how they can obtain the best advantage from the product offered. In exceptional cases (such as those involving "one-off" sales of highly complex machinery which has to be designed and manufactured to customers' specifications) the salesman may even find himself providing technical advice to the managements and designing teams of both the firm he represents and the buyer or potential buyer.

Even the impact of advertising as it has developed, especially over the last 80 years, does not seem to have significantly diminished the importance of the role of the external salesman: for the buyer the proverb "seeing is believing" retains its full import. Fears have also been expressed by certain organisations of travellers

regarding the possible impact of such developments as the growth of
large supermarket chains, which place large orders to their own
specifications directly with manufacturers, and the development of
telephone selling from the selling firm's offices.   However, these
developments do not yet seem to have significantly affected the role
of the commercial traveller.

The method of selling through external salesmen on the basis
of samples is not found in all countries and types of markets.   In
certain developing countries with nascent industries and sellers'
markets, the customers will seek out the manufacturer; he has no
need to go to them.   In countries with centrally planned economies,
where the existence and size of the market for a good is estimated
before production is started, this method of selling is also unneces-
sary (but in Hungary and Poland travellers are still found in small
numbers).   But it is eminently suited to an economy in which enterprises are continually seeking to maintain and expand their markets,
to open up new ones and to get ahead of their competitors, by continually designing and bringing out new or improved products on the
basis of the best market information available and, having produced
a good, then offering it for sale on the open market, with all the
attendant risks inherent in that method of proceeding.

In Japan the manufacturing companies have in recent years
gained a substantial measure of control over the distribution
systems handling their own products, either by acquiring control of
existing wholesalers and retailers or by setting up wholesale and
retail networks of their own.   In sectors such as the cosmetics and
pharmaceutical industries, in which small-scale manufacturers
account for a substantial proportion of total production, the manufacturing firms have joined together to form group marketing sub-
sidiaries to serve retailers directly.   These organisations fulfil
a relatively passive function as a means of channelling goods from
the manufacturer to the consumer, whose custom and loyalty are
sought directly by the manufacturers by means of intensive advertising and sales promotion campaigns.   The exception to this general
rule is to be found in the export trade, much of which is handled
by companies specialising in overseas trading (the Sogo Shosha);
the latter rely heavily on export salesmen working outside the country.

Categories of external salesmen:
clarification of status

Although the basic tasks of all external salesmen are the
same - namely to travel under contract on behalf of one or more
commercial or industrial firms for the purpose of submitting the
products of the firm or firms they represent to customers and of
obtaining orders or closing sales - a number of different categories
may be distinguished.

The largest category today is that of commercial travellers in
the strict sense (often referred to by such titles as "sales representative", "sales agent" or "sales engineer").   They have employee
status and work for a single employer under contracts of service,
organising their work in accordance with their employers'

instructions;[1] while the terms of their remuneration vary, they are in the majority of cases paid a fixed basic salary, expenses and a commission fixed as a proportion of turnover or of the volume of goods sold; and they enjoy the same benefits as other employees as regards such matters as holidays with pay, income security, social security and protection against unfair dismissal.

The situation of commercial travellers as defined contrasts with that of another major group of external salesmen - to which in certain countries the majority of the profession still belongs - namely that of commercial agents. The latter operate not under contracts of employment, but under agency contracts with one or more principals. They have self-employed status, and are thus independent of their principals; they organise their work as they see fit; they may enter into agency contracts with more than one principal; their remuneration consists entirely of commission on orders obtained; they may or may not receive a contribution towards office expenses from their principals; they do not usually fall within the scope of general social security legislation for employees (although in some cases they may be admitted on a voluntary basis); and the termination of their contracts is governed by general contract law.[2] As indicated in the introduction, they fall outside the scope of this study; but in view of their numbers and the similarity of their work and problems to those of certain categories of employee salesmen (and the fact that they are sometimes subject to the same legislation), numerous references will be made to this group.

It can be seen that the status of an external salesman as stipulated in or deriving from his contract can have extremely important consequences of all kinds for him, especially from the standpoints of income and job security. As an employee of the firm for which he works, he can expect to enjoy the benefits of general labour and social legislation and frequently that of collective agreements as well. He will, in the majority of cases, be entitled to a basic salary and to reimbursement of his expenses. He will enjoy the protection of the law against unfair dismissal. He will be entitled to holidays with pay. Even where he is paid entirely through commissions, he will enjoy a measure of income security, when unable to work or unemployed, under sick pay and social insurance or social security schemes.

A commercial agent will be treated as a self-employed person; his income will be entirely dependent on the orders he obtains; he will pay his own expenses; he will in many cases not be covered by the general social security scheme (or at best be admitted on a voluntary basis); and the only safeguards against unfair termination of his contract are likely to be those of ordinary contract law.

---

[1] However, in the United States some firms have instituted plans in which regions and districts are considered as separate enterprises or distributorships and the external sales staff concerned, while retaining employee status, operate with practically all the freedom of action and the responsibility of an independent distributor. See R.E. Sibson: Compensation (New York, AMACOM, 1974), p. 150.

[2] In Spain, however, the term "commercial agent" covers both self-employed persons and persons in an employment relationship.

Between commercial travellers and commercial agents a hybrid category of external salesmen, and the second category with which this study is concerned - referred to throughout the study as "representatives" - has developed. These workers have employee status but may be in contractual relationships with more than one firm; they are paid by commission only, with or without a contribution towards expenses; and, although they have to comply with the instructions of their employers in organising their work (and thus cannot be considered as working on their own account), they often have in practice great freedom in this regard.

Local salesmen or agents, who work in the town or towns in which the firm or firms they represent are situated, may be considered as falling within the category of commercial travellers or that of representatives, since they work under day-to-day supervision.

In the past, considerable difficulties have arisen in determining the status to be accorded to external salesmen generally, and in particular to persons in the last-mentioned group; for, while they had conditions of work similar in many respects to those of commercial agents - and were frequently treated as such by the firms employing them - they could nevertheless argue that, unlike commercial agents, they had no professional personality apart from those of the firms they were representing.

During the inter-war period in particular, in the absence of specific legislation on the subject in many countries, disputes concerning their status - and that of travellers as well - were frequent. For instance, in several of the countries covered by the ILO inquiry undertaken in 1935,[1] numerous cases were reported of travellers being pressed to sign contracts conferring on them the status of independent agents (and thus excluding them from the scope of social insurance schemes and protective labour legislation) but at the same time imposing restrictions on their freedom of action such that their independence was for practical purposes non-existent. Such disputes frequently found their way to the courts, which frequently had to judge them on the basis of legislation drawn up for other purposes (such as industrial and commercial codes, tax laws, etc.),[2] which did not always take into account the peculiar

---

[1] The essential passages of the findings of this inquiry were published in International Labour Review, Vol. XXII, No. 2, Aug. 1935, pp. 208-229; No. 3, Sep. 1935, pp. 374-388; and No. 4, Oct. 1935, pp. 492-504.

[2] The disparity of national situations in this regard even today can be judged from the following: in Bolivia, Brazil, France, Mexico, Ecuador, Panama and Tunisia special provisions on commercial travellers and the like are to be found in the Labour Code; Chile and Uruguay have adopted special legislation, separate from their Labour Codes, to govern the conditions of employment of members of the profession; in Italy and the Netherlands the relevant legislation is found in the Civil Codes, in the Federal Republic of Germany in the Commercial Code and in Switzerland in the Code of Obligations; in Sweden the relevant legislation relates to commissions; in Australia and New Zealand working conditions are regulated by wage awards handed down by industrial conciliation and arbitration commissions; in Austria and Denmark travellers are covered by the general legislation on salaried employees, which contains no special provisions relating to them; while in England and Wales, Canada and the United States they do not appear to form the subject of any special legislation. (The absence of special legislation does not, of course, necessarily mean that travellers and representatives are excluded from the scope of legislation affecting employees generally.)

conditions of work in the profession, and consequently their
judgements did not always carry the desirable degree of legal certainty.

The problem of securing an official definition of the legal
status of external salesmen which would guarantee them the same
social protection as salaried employees in general, while taking
into account their special conditions of employment, was a major
issue within the profession at the time, and the importance
attached to it was reflected in the resolution adopted by the ILO
Advisory Committee on Salaried Employees at its 1935 Session,
quoted earlier.

Since that time a number of countries have adopted legislation
specifying the conditions under which external salesmen are to be
deemed to have the status of employees.[1]   In recent years, too,
the European Commission has reached an advanced stage in its work
on two draft directives, to provide a basis for the harmonisation
of the national legislation of member States on commercial agents
and commercial travellers, with a view to assisting freedom of
establishment and the creation of uniform conditions of competition
throughout the EEC.   The proposals offer elements for a definition
of the two categories, as well as providing a regulatory basis for
the achievement of a certain balance of contractual powers and a
minimum standard of protection for the weaker party.

The main elements conferring employee status on travellers and
representatives - whatever the titles they are given - laid down in
the legislation of the different countries studied are as follows:

1.   The work of the traveller or representative must consist of
     visiting customers to obtain orders (or, in some cases, to
     conclude transactions) for the account of and in the name of
     his employer or employers.   This condition is in force in a
     number of countries (France, Belgium, Federal Republic of
     Germany, Sweden, Switzerland, Peru and others).   The legisla-
     tion in force in Chile, Peru, Switzerland and Uruguay contains
     the specific proviso that it applies only to travellers and
     representatives visiting customers outside their employers'
     establishments;   this provision excludes persons (such as
     medical visitors) who present or demonstrate goods to poten-
     tial customers but do not actually solicit or accept orders,
     and also persons obtaining orders by telephoning from their
     firm's offices.   Sometimes (as in France and Tunisia) there
     is a specific stipulation that, to qualify for employee status,
     a representative must not undertake any operations on his own
     account.   In the Federal Republic of Germany and Switzerland,
     however, he may do so if his employer consents.   In most of
     the countries which have legislation on the point the represen-
     tative may carry on business for a third person if his
     employer consents thereto.

----

[1] Since 1935 new legislation on the subject (sometimes amending
earlier legislation) has been adopted in such countries as Argentina,
Belgium, Brazil, Chile, Ecuador, France, the Federal Republic of
Germany, Mexico, Panama, Peru, Tunisia and Uruguay.

2. The work must be performed on a continuing basis and must be the regular and principal activity of the traveller or representative. Thus, persons performing work of this kind on a part-time or on an occasional basis are excluded. This condition is specifically included in the legislation of France, Mexico and Switzerland and in the draft EEC directive. The commercial travellers' award in force in South Australia sets a minimum travelling period of two-thirds of the traveller's working time every month. There have been cases where the law has a qualifying condition: the performance of representation work to the exclusion of all other types of work. However, experience has shown that such a rigid provision does not always operate to the advantage of the salesman, since cases have occurred where employers have assigned certain ancillary tasks of a non-selling character to their travellers or representatives, thus depriving them of the benefit of the relevant legislation. In France, the legislation concerning commercial travellers and representatives was amended in 1973 to close this loophole.[1]

3. The traveller or representative must carry out his duties in person. Stipulations to this effect are found in Mexico, France and Chile and in the draft EEC directive on commercial travellers. A person who employs others to visit customers on his behalf would thus be excluded, since by doing so he becomes an employer on the same footing as the principal. However, in countries such as the United States salesmen are frequently organised into teams with a leader who, although acting as a supervisor (rather than actually selling) at least part of the time and possibly drawing "override" commissions on the sales of his team-mates, may nevertheless be considered as a salesman.

4. The traveller or representative must be bound by a contract stipulating the nature of the goods or services to be offered for sale, the region of activity or the group of customers to be visited, and the rate of remuneration (France, Tunisia).

5. The traveller's or representative's powers are normally confined to the seeking of orders. He is thus not normally allowed to make physical sales except where the nature of the goods offered (e.g. gold- and silverware) is such as to make sale on a sample basis impossible (although in some countries he may be given responsibility for physical delivery and empowered to collect moneys due). In addition, the orders he receives in response to his offers for sale do not of themselves constitute a conclusion of contracts of sale; except where the traveller or representative has special authorisation to conclude transactions binding on his employer, the orders are subject to the latter's acceptance. In Italy, however, travellers making physical sales are covered by the relevant collective agreements.

The severity of the qualifying conditions varies from country to country. Thus, for instance, in France a traveller or representative who does not satisfy the first four conditions mentioned is

---

[1] H.P. Le Ferme: "La Loi", in La Tribune Libre (Paris), No. 257, Mar. 1977, p. 3.

not entitled to the benefit of the special legislation concerning the profession;[1] while at the other extreme, in Argentina and Ecuador, all commercial agents, as well as travellers, effecting sales for the account of individuals or corporate bodies are deemed to be in private employ provided that they act not at their own risk, but at that of one or more principals.

Although substantial progress has thus been made in a number of countries towards the definition of the legal status of travellers and representatives as regards their entitlement to employee status, difficulties frequently arise concerning the determination of whether the relationship between a traveller or representative and his principal is one of employment or not. In particular, cases frequently occur in which contracts which bear the designation of "agency contracts" have in fact many of the characteristics of contracts of employment. The legislation applicable to commercial travellers and representatives in several countries (France, Belgium, Brazil) specifically provides that such designations shall not affect the status of the contract as a contract of employment provided that the other conditions applicable are met; while in other countries (such as Argentina, Federal Republic of Germany, Switzerland), under general legislation, the content of the agreement takes precedence over its title. In such cases the courts, in seeking to determine the intentions of the parties, have taken into account such factors as the following:

(a) whether the salesman works for one firm or several. In England and Wales, the Netherlands and Sweden, for example, a traveller may not work for more than one employer at the same time and in Switzerland the Joint Committee on the Status of Commercial Travellers has ruled that a traveller should not represent more than one firm save in exceptional cases. However, in most other countries he may work for several employers (subject to the agreement of all of them) without losing the right to employee status.

(b) whether and to what extent he is required to carry out the instructions of the firm he represents in organising and performing his work. Such instructions may relate to the customers or area to be visited, the itinerary to be followed, the types of goods to be sold, the relative priority to be given to promoting the sales of the different lines of goods offered, the provision of regular reports on his activities and on the state of the market, etc. This is one of the most difficult criteria to assess. While there is general acceptance that commercial agents act in full independence, the situations of travellers and representatives range from subjection to detailed instructions and close supervision to a de facto independence on a par with that of an independent agent. Such independence offers grounds for the assertion that they should be treated as self-employed agents, since it can be argued that the nature of their work is such that the supervisory functions their employers can exercise over them are so tenuous as to make it impossible for a genuine employer-employee relationship to exist.

---

[1] The French courts have on occasion refused to concede the status of representative to a person with a contract entitled "representative's contract" where these conditions are not satisfied. See Recueil Dalloz-Sirey (Paris), 1973, Informations rapides, p. 38.

In this connection the courts in Italy have taken the line that a person designated as a commercial agent cannot be considered as enjoying independence (considered an essential factor in an agency contract) if he has to follow an itinerary laid down by his principal, to visit customers designated by the principal and to complete his tour within a time limit set by the principal.[1]   Conversely, a Belgian court has ruled that the fact that a traveller is not bound to follow the instructions of the firm he represents, and is only required to report orders taken, may be considered as evidence that he is not an employee.[2]   On the other hand, the Court of Cassation in the same country has ruled that an employment relationship may exist between a person offering his services for hire and the person hiring them even where the authority of the latter is not exercised continuously or even not at all.[3]   In France, the requirement of the existence of a master-and-servant relationship of authority and subordination between an employer and a sales representative was abolished by the Act of 18 July 1937, which for the first time gave representatives seeking orders for more than one firm - who had previously been treated as independent commercial agents - access to employee status.[4]

(c)   whether he receives a regular, fixed salary, or whether he is paid on commission only.   In Italy, for instance, a traveller paid by commission only is not deemed to be an employee;[5]   in other countries, such as France, Mexico and Switzerland, whereas the payment of a regular wage or salary creates a presumption of the existence of a contract of employment, the fact that payment is made by commission only does not disprove the existence of such a contract.   The existence of provision for payment of a minimum guaranteed amount every month, either as salary or in the form of an advance on future commissions if the commission earned in any one month falls short of the stipulated minimum, may also be taken as evidence of the existence of a contract of employment.

(d)   whether his expenses are reimbursed.   Where this is not the case, or the traveller only receives a lump-sum contribution to his office expenses, this may be treated as evidence that he does not have employee status.   On the other hand, the inclusion of an allowance for expenses in the rate of commission might prove the existence of an employment relationship.

---

[1] Cimmino e Getici: Compendio de legislazione sociale (Emola, Galeati, 1967), p. 448.

[2] Journal des Tribunaux du Travail (Brussels, Larcier), 30 April 1978.

[3] See R. Bourgeois and E. Van Put: "Le Statut de représentant du commerce est-il dérogatoire au droit commun?" in Revue de Droit Social, 1970, No. 4, pp. 145-156.

[4] J. Michot: "Le statut professionnel", in La Tribune Libre, No. 257, Mar. 1977, pp. 25-38.

[5] Cimmino e Getici, op. cit., p. 454.

(e)   other factors, such as whether he has to have a trader's
      licence;   whether he does any work for his own account;
      whether he employs other persons;   whether he has to make his
      own arrangements for payment of social security contributions
      and value-added tax;   whether he has his own offices and uses
      his own letterhead for correspondence;   and whether he uses
      order forms bearing his own letterhead or that of his princi-
      pal.

      In addition, in a few countries the legislature or the courts
have sought to protect the traveller or representative by establishing a presumption of employee status, laying the burden of proof of
the contrary on the employer or declaring invalid certain procedures
which, if allowed, would deprive the traveller of the protection
afforded by that status.   Thus, section 154 of the proposed Labour
Code for Bolivia provides that a person paid solely on a commission
basis shall be deemed to have employee status unless the contrary
is proved.   In France, under section 791-1 of the Labour Code,
which relates specifically to the status of commercial travellers
and representatives, all contracts which fulfil the necessary conditions are deemed to be contracts for the hire of services, notwithstanding any provision they contain to the contrary.   The Belgian
Act of 3 July 1978 on contracts of employment contains a similar
provision.   Similarly, in Brazil, section 10 of the Act of 18 July
1957 states that any person performing the functions of a traveller
or representative shall be deemed to be in an employment relationship with his principal, whatever his designation or job title.
(Provisions of this kind protect a person engaged in representation
from a claim that his contract is not a contract of employment on
the grounds that in it he is designated as, for instance, a commercial agent.)   French law also has a provision to the effect that
even persons performing representation work without a written contract shall be deemed to fall within the scope of the law (earlier
legislation required written contracts).

      In some countries, too, the courts have handed down decisions
the effect of which is to give the traveller or representative protection against certain types of challenges to his claim for
employee status.   Thus, for instance, the labour court in Mons
(Belgium), in a judgement dated 13 April 1970, ruled that the presumption that a representative's contract was a contract of employment was not invalidated by the fact that the representative was
paid solely in the form of commissions on the basis of stamped
vouchers drawn up in accordance with the statutory provisions applicable to commercial agents;   that he did not pay social security
contributions;   that he was not a member of a union;   or that he was
a member of the family allowances scheme for self-employed persons,
since those factors were not relevant for the purpose of establishing whether a relationship of subordination to authority existed.[1]

      Inevitably, however, difficulties arise in securing the appli-
cation of the law in individual cases.   An external salesman working under an agency contract who feels that the terms of his contractual relationship entitle him to employee status will understandably feel hesitant to approach his principal on the subject or

---

[1] Judgement summarised in Revue de droit social (Brussels),
1970, No. 4, p. 172.

to envisage instituting court proceedings to secure that status - at least, while the contractual relationship lasts. However, cases have been encountered where a worker in this situation has, on termination of the relationship, applied to the courts for a ruling that his conditions of employment were such as to entitle him to employee status with a view to obtaining the termination benefits due to an employee and the payment by the firm of employer social security contributions in respect of the period covered by the relationship.

The most radical stand encountered on the question of employee status for commercial representatives is that taken by the General Union of Workers in Spain. In comments made in 1978 on proposed new legislation concerning commercial travellers, it recommended that they and commercial agents should be treated alike in labour law, since in the majority of cases they were performing the same functions and were paid in the same way, and that frequently the external sales forces of individual companies included persons who were registered commercial agents and persons who were not.

Numbers of persons engaged in external sales

Determining the number of persons engaged in external sales work is not an easy task. Published national employment statistics, which are usually broken down by sector of activity rather than by occupation, rarely contain separate figures for travellers and representatives, and it is necessary to look elsewhere to find information on the subject.

One useful source of information is population censuses. While these do not reflect the most recent situation (most of them having been conducted at the beginning of the decade) and do not always even give separate figures for the numbers of persons in the category (including them, for instance, under the general heading of "commerce"), some of them nevertheless provide figures which give at least an approximate idea of the situation today in the countries concerned. Another useful source available in some countries are the statistics produced by occupational social security schemes and, in one or two cases, the findings of inquiries, official and unofficial.

While the figures obtained in these different ways are not always strictly comparable, they do enable an approximate idea to be obtained of the size of the profession within the economically active population as a whole.

Thus, in Australia the June 1971 census revealed that there were 49,327 commercial travellers and manufacturers' agents (46,816 men and 2,511 women) in an economically active population of some 5.3 million. In Belgium in 1970, out of a total economically active population of 3.52 million, the census revealed a total of 37,221 travellers, representatives and local agents (34,987 men and 2,234 women), of whom 3,271 were independent. The Brazil population census of the same year gave figures of 111,607 (105,200 men and 6,407 women) travellers and local agents and 37,800 commercial agents (32,239 men and 5,561 women) in an economically active population of 29.5 million. In Denmark, in an economically active population of 2.3 million there are reckoned to be some 18,000 external salesmen.

In the Federal Republic of Germany, the 1970 census found, in an economically active population of 26.6 million, a total of 190,000 travellers and representatives (170,100 men and 19,900 women), of whom 77,100 were self-employed and 112,900 employed. The census held in Spain during the same year gave a total of 135,538 persons (129,946 men and 5,592 women) classified as "commercial agents and travellers" in a total economically active population of 11.9 million; of these, 102,000 were "working for a fixed wage or salary or on commission", but it is not clear how many of these had employee status. Lastly, in the United States, under the two headings "sales representatives, manufacturing" and "sales representatives, wholesale" in the 1970 census (i.e. persons selling physical goods), there appeared a total of 1,066,912 persons (986,883 men and 80,029 women) out of a total economically active population of 82.9 million. (To this total should be added an unknown number - possibly of the order of 100,000 - of travellers and representatives in the services sector.)

In five out of these seven countries the group of persons engaged in sales representation work represented in 1970 or 1971 approximately 1 per cent of the economically active population, and thus constituted a group roughly comparable in size with the group of employees in the electricity, gas and water sector, and in a sixth (Denmark) 0.8 per cent. In the seventh (Brazil) the group represented approximately 0.5 per cent of the economically active population, but it is generally recognised to be expanding rapidly as the country's economic development gathers pace and levels of prosperity rise.

In other industrialised countries, a somewhat similar situation prevails. In Great Britain the sample surveys of economic activity undertaken within the framework of the 1971 census revealed that the category "commercial travellers and manufacturers' agents" comprised slightly more than 200,000 men and approximately 10,000 women, out of a total economically active population of approximately 25 million; in the Netherlands the percentage is about 1.0 (50,000 out of an economically active population of some 5 million). In Italy, it was estimated at the end of 1978 that, out of an economically active population of approximately 20 million, there were some 400,000 persons exercising the profession, of whom about 300,000 had the status of commercial agents. In Austria and Switzerland, the percentages are somewhat lower - about 0.7 per cent - but the figures available do not include commercial agents. Lastly, in France, with an economically active population of some 22 million, it is estimated on the basis of statistics from the complementary pensions scheme for the profession and privately conducted surveys, that there were at the end of 1977 approximately 154,000 travellers and representatives with employee status and covered by the professional statute; it is believed that there are at least as many again who are salaried employees but do not enjoy the special privileges conferred by the statute.

The foregoing suffices to show that, in a number of industrialised countries at any rate, commercial travellers, representatives and agents form a substantial group within the economically active population. Two other features are also worthy of note: the variations in the respective proportions of commercial travellers and representatives and of commercial agents in the total number of persons identified as engaged in sales representation work in the countries for which separate figures have been available; and the small proportion of women in the totals, again where separate figures have been available (10.4 per cent in the Federal Republic of Germany, 7.5 per cent in the United States, 5 per cent or less in Australia, Belgium, Brazil, Great Britain and Spain). The proportion appears to be particularly low in technical sales.

Employment trends

In the absence of yearly figures concerning the numbers of travellers and representatives in employment, it is not easy to distinguish trends in employment levels with any degree of statistical certainty, and one is obliged to resort to estimates made by governments and by employers' and workers' organisations. Thus, for instance, certain unions in Belgium and France consider that the numbers of travellers and representatives have remained fairly stable in recent years; in Thailand their numbers appear to have risen. In Switzerland, where detailed year-by-year figures are available, the numbers of travellers seeking orders from firms and institutions fell from 21,614 in 1967 to 16,775 in 1977 - a fall of 22 per cent; but half of the total fall occurred in 1971; the effects of the recession which began in 1974 on the numbers of persons in this group appears to have been relatively small. In Brazil and Ecuador the governmental authorities are of the view that the profession is expanding with the over-all expansion of the economy. In the United States, employment prospects in sales representation of both manufacturers and wholesalers were expected in 1975 to be good, with the numbers of jobs increasing until well into the 1980s; this was attributed to economic and population growth, and also to the need to lay more emphasis on selling activities, in particular to cope adequately with intensifying competition.[1]

Equally little information on unemployment trends can be found in published figures where, as was the case for employment, unemployed commercial travellers and representatives are frequently classified within larger occupational groups.

However, where figures are available, they suggest that unemployment within the profession is not significantly more than the average for the economically active population as a whole. Thus, in England and Wales in March 1978, unemployment among commercial travellers and representatives was of the order of 6.5 per cent, as against approximately 6 per cent among the economically active population as a whole.[2] A similar situation is found in the Netherlands in October 1978, where the corresponding figures are of the order of 4 per cent.[3] In both countries the numbers of unemployed have varied during the last few years, roughly in accordance with the general level of employment. On the other hand, in Austria the trade union for salaried employees in private employment is of the opinion that unemployment among travellers and representatives has risen less than among other categories of workers in recent years; it attributes this to the fact that the increased competition caused by the current recession has compelled employers to increase their selling efforts. The view is also held within the union that unemployment within the profession is very low (although cases of termination of their contracts by their

---

[1] US Department of Labor, Bureau of Labor Statistics: Occupational Outlook Handbook, 1974-75 edition, pp. 230 ff.

[2] See Department of Employment Gazette, Aug. 1978, p. 930.

[3] See Sociale Maandstatistiek, Dec. 1978.

employers are frequent) on account of the exceptional versatility
of travellers. (In this connection, the possibility that certain
travellers and representatives who become redundant in external
sales are transferred to other jobs within the same establishment
cannot be ignored.) The principal commercial travellers' union
in Denmark reports a similar situation there: although unemployment in recent years has been high (of the order of 5-6 per cent
of membership), the levels of unemployment in many other trades are
twice as high as that in external selling. Lastly, in the Federal
Republic of Germany, even during the recession years 1975-77, there
were never more than a few hundred travellers and representatives
registered as unemployed.

On the other hand, the unions in several countries state that
recently a growing tendency has been observed among employers to
seek to induce their employee travellers to exchange their contracts of service for commercial agency contracts. This enables
them to pay solely on the basis of commission on orders actually
taken, and in some cases to escape the burden of employer social
security contributions as well, without weakening their sales
forces. An extreme case in this regard appears to be Italy, where
one union estimates that during the last ten years the numbers of
travellers and representatives with employee status has fallen from
150,000 to 80,000 or thereabouts, while the numbers of independent
agents and representatives has risen from 120,000 to 300,000, many
of them having little or no job security or even working clandes-
tinely. It also observes that very few commercial travellers and
representatives reach retirement age as such.

There are certainly factors present today which would seem to
make for a fall in the demand for travellers and representatives,
particularly at the wholesale level. They arise in particular
from amalgamations of supplier firms; strengthening of the market
position of the biggest firms (such as chain stores and purchasing
groups), which can negotiate directly with a producing firm, often
from a dominant position; and from the ensuing disappearance of
smaller stores and, subsequently, of their suppliers. The expansion of the use of computers in sales work may also have had effects
on employment.

However, notwithstanding these factors - and also the present
recession, which has brought about substantial general rises in
unemployment in most countries - the scant evidence available
suggests that, at the worst, unemployment among travellers and
representatives is not increasing any faster than unemployment in
general; that in a number of countries their numbers are remaining
stable; and that in the United States and certain developing countries there even appear to be prospects for expansion. While any
attempt to explain this trend must inevitably involve a degree of
conjecture, it seems reasonably safe to say that one contributory
factor is the heightening of competition for markets, currently
aggravated by the need to maintain sales during the recession.
This factor underlines once again the importance of the role of
commercial travellers and representatives in the machinery of trade
and distribution.

CHAPTER II

TRADE UNIONS AND PROFESSIONAL ASSOCIATIONS
WITHIN THE PROFESSION

In all countries in which commercial travellers and representatives have employee status, they enjoy, by virtue of that status, the same rights with regard to freedom of association and the right to organise as other categories of workers.

However, the percentage of travellers and representatives who are union members, while varying from country to country, frequently tends to be lower than among workers in general. In Australia about 30 per cent are unionised (as against about 50 per cent of the total labour force); in the Netherlands estimates vary between 25 and 30 per cent (40 per cent in the total labour force); in the Federal Republic of Germany and Austria the figures are about 15 per cent (39 per cent and 58 per cent respectively); in the United Kingdom about 10 per cent are union members (43 per cent); while the figure for the United States is of the order of 2 per cent only (22 per cent).[1]

On the other hand, in France it is estimated that some 50 per cent of commercial travellers and representatives with special status as such belong to unions - well over the level of unionisation of the labour force as a whole (23 per cent); in Sweden and Denmark it is estimated that 70 to 80 per cent of travellers and representatives are union members (about the same proportion as in the labour force as a whole), while in Poland and Hungary practically all of them are. In some countries (such as New Zealand) union membership is compulsory save where commission accounts for more than half of remuneration. In Western Australia the Commercial Travellers' Award of 1975 (No. 35) appears to provide for a kind of "closed shop", under which a commercial traveller who is not a union member may be required to apply for membership and has a right of appeal if his application is refused.

Unions of commercial travellers and representatives as such are relatively rare. The general tendency among those who do become union members is to join a national union covering a larger group of employees, such as employees in commerce or salaried employees in general. Frequently they have a choice of unions which they may join within the country; thus in Sweden they may join the Swedish Industrial Salaried Employees' Federation, the Swedish Union of Commercial Employees or the Swedish Association of Travelling Representatives; while in France and Italy, where there are several trade union federations with different political leanings, commercial travellers and representatives are found in all of them.[2]

---

[1] The percentages of union members in the labour force are drawn from different sources and based on different years and are given as approximations only.

[2] Many of them also belong to the General Confederation of Supervisory Staff (CGC), which has the largest number of travellers and representatives within its membership.

These unions generally have separate sections to deal with the special problems of travellers and representatives. There are, however, some countries in which there are separate unions for commercial travellers and representatives only; this is the case, for instance, in Chile and Denmark, and also in Great Britain, where the United Commercial Travellers' Association, although it recently amalgamated with a larger union, still retains substantial independence.

The fact that some of these unions also accept commercial agents as members is further evidence of the closeness of the relationship between the two professions.[1]

While affiliation to a larger trade union grouping does strengthen the position of travellers and representatives in a number of respects (in particular by reason of the union's presence within the individual undertaking), it can on occasion have disadvantages for them where the union is unable fully to appreciate their special problems. In New Zealand, for instance, the compulsory affiliation of commercial travellers to the district storemen and packers' unions has given rise to some contention on these grounds, and moves are under way to establish a separate union for the profession. However, complaints of this kind appear to be rare.

In some countries the organisations formed by commercial travellers and representatives appear to be more of a professional than a trade union character. This is the case, for instance, with the Swiss Society of Commercial Travellers and the Colleges of Commercial Agents in Spain. Organisations of this kind pursue the defence of the interests of the profession and frequently offer a wide range of services to their members, but do not participate directly in collective bargaining. It is not infrequent for a traveller who is a member of a union to be also a member of a professional association.

In selecting the services which they will offer to travellers and representatives, the commercial travellers' unions (or the specialised sections for travellers in larger unions) have to take into account the peculiar features of the profession and of conditions of employment in it - the intersectoral character of the profession, covering as it does a wide range of industries and services; the relatively small numbers of travellers and representatives employed by any one firm; the fact that travellers and representatives are often employed under individual contracts of employment, the terms of which often differ from one to another; and the isolated character of the work of their members, many of whom live and work away from their employer's premises and only appear there occasionally.

This last factor makes the task of the unions catering for commercial travellers and representatives particularly difficult. Since they work away from the premises of the firms employing them and come there only rarely, the union representatives in the firm

---

[1] The membership of the United Commercial Travellers' Association of Great Britain includes commercial agents; while that of the Colleges of Commercial Agents in Spain includes travellers and representatives with employee status. In Italy, the membership of the three principal unions catering for employee travellers and representatives also includes commercial agents; two of these unions are signatories to the 1978 national agreement concerning independent commercial agents and representatives.

have a harder job to maintain regular contact with them than with
other categories of workers, who work on the employer's premises;
in addition, where they are entitled to representation within joint
machinery such as works councils, it may be difficult to represent
them adequately.   Similarly, since they often live and work in
isolation from the rest of the labour force and from one another,
it is often difficult to bring them together to discuss common
problems.   These difficulties can be compounded by the fact that
large numbers of travellers and representatives do not join unions,
and also where a single firm has both employees and self-employed
persons within its external sales force.

Thus in the unions catering for travellers and representatives
there is a tendency to lay emphasis on the provision of services
tailored to the needs of the individual, over and above those services available to the membership in general.

Legal advice and assistance to the individual occupies a
particularly important place in the range of special services
offered.   Thus, a union will advise a traveller or representative
who so requests, in the negotiation of the terms of his individual
contract of employment;   draw attention to clauses which appear
unfair in individual contracts and advise on ways and means of
securing modifications;   and advise and assist generally in disputes
regarding employee rights, especially in matters of termination.[1]
For these purposes it will if necessary approach the employer
directly;   where the approach fails to produce an acceptable solution
the union may advise on or actually handle all necessary conciliation
or legal proceedings.   Direct industrial action in furtherance of
a dispute appears to be extremely rare.

The volume of advice and assistance provided can be considerable.
In France, for instance, during 1978 the legal department of the
Central National Trade Union Organisation for Commercial Travellers
and Representatives gave advice to over 8,500 persons (out of a
total membership of some 45,000) and had a pending file of some
3,000 cases in which the union was either negotiating with an
employer or conducting court proceedings.   In Switzerland, in 1978,
the Swiss Society of Commercial Travellers, which has an active
membership of some 10,000, gave 2,408 consultations to members.
The principal subjects raised were: analysis of contracts or contract clauses, 28 per cent;   reimbursement of expenses, 22 per cent;
pay, commission, bonuses, etc., 14 per cent;   improper termination,
14 per cent;   social insurance and unfair competition, 8 per cent
each.

Other services provided by unions for commercial travellers
and representatives may include negotiation with the competent
authorities on tax and social security problems;   the organisation
of training courses;   the circulation of vacancy notices;   a mort-
gage loan or guarantee service;   the securing of special discounts
on insurance premiums and hotel charges;   welfare services to deal
with cases of special hardship;   and the administration of special
insurance schemes, especially of a provident character.

---

[1] In Denmark, for instance, the principal commercial travellers'
union succeeded during the period 1974-78 in having some 60 radius
clauses declared invalid, either by negotiation or by legal proceedings.

General problems, affecting equally all members of the profession, are sometimes dealt with by negotiation with the national apex organisations of employers on a sectoral or an intersectoral basis; where necessary, the unions concerned associate to take part in the negotiations.

In France, for instance, the national employers' confederation and the unions of travellers and representatives concluded in 1975 a collective agreement covering certain problems specific to the profession, such as minimum earnings, sick pay, termination benefits and the radius clause.   The approach adopted by the negotiating parties is illustrated by the following passage in the preamble to the agreement:

> The contracting parties,
>
> ...
>
> Observing that the problems of commercial travellers and representatives are specific and cannot be systematically treated as identical with any other category of staff, firstly, on account of the actual nature of their work and of their conditions of employment in the different branches of industry and commerce, and secondly because they are situated at widely differing levels in the hierarchy,
>
> Have decided to deal with these problems on a national interoccupational basis, without reference to other categories of employees.   ...

In Italy there are two collective agreements in force, covering all aspects of conditions of employment of travellers, representatives and local agents in commerce and in industry respectively; they were signed by the competent national employers' organisations and, on the union side, jointly by representatives of all the main trade union federations.   However, the trade union federations for commerce employees, which cater for travellers employed in commerce, has proposed that the latter be brought within a single collective agreement covering all commerce employees, with special clauses to cover their special problems.[1]   In Norway the Commercial Employers' Association has concluded collective agreements with the national association of commercial travellers covering a wide range of conditions of employment; these agreements follow the main lines of those in existence for commercial and office employees generally, adapting their provisions where necessary to take account of the special conditions of employment of commercial travellers.   In Switzerland there is standing joint machinery for negotiation between the apex employers' organisations and the organisations representing travellers on the latter's conditions of employment; it publishes guidelines (which are widely followed) on such matters as pay; expenses; holidays with pay; remuneration when prevented from working for reasons such as sickness, accident or jury or military service; termination indemnities; pension insurance; the consequences of rationalisation measures; vocational training; and car costs and insurance.

---

[1] Federazione unitaria lavoratori comercio turismo servizi: Piattaforma rivendicative per il CCNL dei dipendenti da "aziende commerciali", adopted by the National Assembly of Commerce Workers on 11-12 September 1979 (Turin, mimeographed).

Lastly, the organisations representing commercial travellers and representatives frequently negotiate with the competent government authorities on such matters as the treatment of expenses for tax purposes, parking concessions in large cities, exemption from vehicle taxes, etc. They may also operate public relations services to present the position of their members on various matters to the general public, the legislature, and other groups.

CHAPTER III

PREPARATION FOR THE PROFESSION:
CAREER DEVELOPMENT

Image of the profession

The profession of commercial traveller or representative today
is an extremely heterogeneous one. Firstly, it cuts across most
sectors of production and services, with each sector having its own
specific marketing methods and requirements. Secondly, the
different levels of selling involved range from the collection of
stocking-up orders from retail shops (with the occasional demonstration of a new product) to the negotiation of the purchase of high-
technology goods, possibly requiring adaptation to the needs of the
customer, in the face of fierce competition on specifications and
cost from other firms.

In view of this situation, it is practically impossible to
state that the profession of commercial traveller stands at any
particular level in the occupational hierarchy. At the lower end
of the range, the duties may be mainly of a routine character; at
the upper end, an external salesman may be advising top management
directly. It is equally impossible to lay down any uniform pattern of academic qualifications or experience for entry into the
profession.

There is, however, widespread agreement on the personality
characteristics required of a commercial traveller. He is expected
to have an outgoing, sociable personality, be able to communicate
easily with other persons and inspire confidence. He must be of
an independent disposition, able to operate alone, to plan his own
work and to exercise his judgement. Since he is not under supervision, he requires a high degree of self-discipline. Lastly, he
will need considerable mental resilience - an ability to overcome
hostility, to absorb objections as challenges, to live with
repeated rejection (for in most cases only a minority of visits
result in the placing of orders) and to persevere in difficult
cases. Above all, he must be able to act as a worthy representative of the firm employing him; for he will frequently be the
customer's only contact with the firm.

The conventional "profile" of commercial travellers and
representatives has evolved considerably since they first emerged
as an occupational group.

The early travelling salesmen - a prototype of whom may be
found in Balzac's Illustre Gaudissart - used sales techniques akin
to those of itinerant pedlars, seeking to win customers by artfully
directed argument, often playing on the psychology of the customer
as much as they demonstrated the usefulness of their wares. It
was salesmen of this kind who contributed much to the development
of the traditional, stereotyped image of the travelling salesman -
a man "riding on a smile and a shoeshine", as Arthur Miller put it,
working a route of small country towns and villages, aggressively
pushing for orders of his lines of goods, concerned primarily with
earning as much commission as possible, with a facile tongue, a
ready wit and a fund of stories, on tour for weeks or even months

at a stretch, living in cheap hotels, drinking and gambling to pass away his spare time.

Although this traditional image still remains deeply rooted in the popular imagination, in recent times radical changes have taken place in the nature of external sales work and in the qualities and standards of behaviour required of its practitioners.[1]

These changes have been in large measure a response to developments in the market. Customers have become more professional in the assessment of their requirements; the technical considerations governing these requirements have become more specific and more complex; and competition to win sales and sales outlets is constantly increasing. The need to maintain and expand sales in the face of these developments has given rise to considerable changes in the responsibilities of salesmen and the approaches required of them. It is no longer sufficient to make a one-time sale; a customer won must be kept, often in the face of competition from other salesmen seeking to win him away again. Thus the salesman must not only persuade the customer that his product best meets the customer's requirements; he must also develop a relationship of trust between the customer and the firm he represents - possibly even formalised as a franchise agreement - for every business needs a foundation of steady, repeat customers to remain viable. He must therefore be particularly sensitive to customer requirements, problems, habits, preferences, and even prejudices, and be prepared to offer his and his firm's assistance in meeting them - to be as concerned about the profitability of his customer's firm as he is about that of his own. Much depends on the personality of the salesman in this regard, for a single faux pas may cost him and his firm a valued customer; and much has been written on strategies designed to enable salesmen to cope with these new developments.[2]

These new demands on salesmen have affected their employment situations and the qualifications required of them in a number of ways.

For instance, a salesman selling highly technical products for use in industrial processes (such as electronic instruments or machine tools) must not only have a thorough knowledge of the technical aspects of his own firm's products; he must also be able to appreciate the technical problems of the customer's own process and markets. He may have to co-operate with the research and development department of his own firm in finding ways of adapting a product to the customer's needs; to train the customer's employees in the operation and maintenance of the new equipment; and to make return visits to ensure that it is giving the desired service. A

---

[1] This image has been reinforced by recent literature; mention may be made, among popular writings in the United States alone, of Eugene O'Neill: The Iceman Cometh (1946); Arthur Miller: Death of a Salesman (1949); and Robert Tallant: Southern Territory (1951). On the subject of the persistence of this image, see Donald L. Thompson: "Stereotype of the Salesman", in Harvard Business Review, Jan.-Feb. 1972, pp. 20 ff.

[2] See, for instance, M. Hanan, J. Cribbin and H. Heiser: Consultative Selling, revised edition (New York, American Management Associations, 1973).

salesman of this kind will often need higher education or advanced technical training in addition to his selling skills (in practice technical salesmen are frequently drawn from the technical staff of the firms they represent) and will be closely integrated into the staff of his company, where he may have the support of a market research department in seeking out new customers.

A salesman of consumer goods selling to retail customers, either for a manufacturer or for a wholesaler, will have different tasks.   The goods he offers for sale are usually standardised, and he is consequently unlikely to be directly involved in production adaptation (although passing back customer comments on the goods offered is a normal part of his work).   He is thus unlikely to need such a high standard of technical knowledge as a technical salesman, and may be able to work with a considerable degree of independence, representing several manufacturers - although he will not offer lines of goods competing with one another without the consent of his employers or principals.   (The situation of a whole-saler's representative in this regard is somewhat different;   to ensure a comprehensive service to retailers he is obliged to have on offer a choice of items;   his interest is rather to be able to respond fully and promptly to his customers' requests than to promote the sale of a particular line of goods.)   The additional services he may provide include imparting information on the general market situation and trends;   assisting with stock checking; suggesting improvements in stock control systems;   giving advice on advertising, pricing and displays;   and, where the product is a technical one (such as air conditioners), make suggestions on installation and maintenance.

There is, however, one fundamental feature of the situation of the commercial traveller or representative which has remained unchanged.   To an external salesman the interests of the customer are of more direct concern than to other employees in the firm he represents.   For this reason his level of commitment to the firm and its objectives may be lower than that of other employees;[1] alternatively, influenced by customer needs and attitudes, he may interpret the stated objectives of the company in a different manner from his sales manager.

The difficulty of maintaining adequate understanding and commitment is likely to be aggravated where the salesman has his base in the territory in which he works, isolated from his colleagues and visited only occasionally by a supervisor and thus able to maintain communications with his head office only on an intermittent basis by correspondence or infrequent visits.   This situation creates problems both for an employer seeking to strengthen the loyalty of his external sales force and for the salesman himself in situations where his interests - both as a representative of the firm and as an employee - are liable to be affected.

---

[1] See David W. Belcher: Compensation administration (prentice-Hall, Englewood Cliffs, N.J., 1974), p. 521.

Preparation for the exercise of the profession

Knowledge and personality requirements

As was seen earlier, one fundamental difference between the profession of commercial traveller or representative and other occupations calling for similar levels of knowledge and responsibility lies in its diversity; commercial travellers and representatives are not confined within a given sector or group of sectors, but are found in nearly all industries producing goods and services.   The same may, of course, be said of certain other professions, such as personnel management; but that function tends to develop a hierarchical structure within each firm in which it exists, whereas travellers and representatives, notwithstanding the variety of levels of responsibility at which they operate, tend to form a single stratum within the sales and marketing organisation of a given firm.   Thus, the structure of the profession, if presented diagrammatically, would be relatively flat.

This diversity and flatness complicates preparation for the profession.

Many occupations are so structured that a young person at school can decide that he or she will take up a particular occupation and thereafter orientate his education and vocational training so as to give himself the best possible preparation for it; thus when he obtains his first job he will have at least a theoretical basis which only needs to be rounded out by experience.   The situation is somewhat different in external selling.

One reason for this difference is to be found in the wide variety of types of knowledge (of which selling methods are only one) which a traveller needs in order to do his job well.   Much of this knowledge cannot be acquired during education.

First, the newcomer has to acquire a thorough knowledge of the product he is to sell, its uses, its qualities and its shortcomings and its possible adaptations, and of the products of his competitors. The higher the level of technology incorporated in the product, the more thorough his understanding of it will need to be.   This knowledge can only be acquired in the enterprise through an actual study of the product itself in a work context (although a university or technical education will in some cases be essential for proper understanding).   In addition, he needs a thorough knowledge of the company's marketing policies and procedures in relation to such matters as delivery, credit, pricing, accounts collection and servicing.   This knowledge, too, can only be acquired within the enterprise.

The importance of this knowledge for a traveller becomes apparent when one remembers that, for the great majority of goods and services, sales are made on the basis of interviews, in which the salesman is on his own with the prospective customer and unable to call on the assistance of other departments of his firm.   If his presentation fails to convince, the sale is likely to be lost. If he knows all the facts, he can make an adequate presentation specifically adapted to the needs or problems of the customer; give specific, accurate answers to questions, without having to take refuge in generalisations; and thus dispel the concern about the suitability of the product and the reliability of the selling firm which a prospective new customer is likely to have.

Secondly, he has to acquire a thorough knowledge of the sector
of the economy in which he is working, of the market and of individual customers - the problems of their own businesses, their wants
(and their own customers' wants) and even their prejudices.   He
has to be constantly in contact with the customers, keeping his
knowledge of their wants up to date.   He has to be continually on
the alert for changes in the nature of demand, of shifts away from
one type of goods to another.   He has to be on the look-out for
products competing, or liable to compete, with those he sells, to
be able to evaluate their chances of success and possibly suggest
to his employer means of making his own product more competitive.
This knowledge can only be acquired by continuous and direct contact
with the market and with the customers - again, in the context of
actual work.

A third type of knowledge required relates to the actual
methods of selling.   Attention centres here on the organisation of
selling interviews - territory analysis, the choice of prospects;
preparation for and conduct of the interview; effective communication and clear exposition; dealing with objections; adjusting
sales propositions to consumer needs; after-sales service and
dealing with complaints; and self-analysis.

Much has been written on techniques of selling, and many
training courses have been organised, either by individual companies
for their own external sales staff, by specialised private agencies
or by the public authorities.   However, many travellers and
representatives have never attended courses on this subject, relying
on trial and error to develop their selling techniques.

This can to some extent be explained by reference to the
personal attitudes and the motivation of those who decide to make
selling a career.

In external selling, where success depends to a great extent
on the rapport which the salesman develops with the customer,
motivation and personality factors are of special importance.
Employers, when interviewing prospective newcomers to the profession, attach particular importance to personality characteristics;
their approach is frequently that, once the right kind of person
has been found, he can be given any necessary training, but that no
amount of training can make a good salesman out of a person with an
unsuitable personality - in other words, that "salesmen are born,
not made".   Thus a person who enters the profession may well have
the basic talents needed for selling - described earlier - and
achieve a measure of early success without undergoing formal training in selling techniques.

Many people do enter working life with the intention of taking
up a selling career; but this is by no means always so.   Cases are
frequently quoted of experienced employees in a firm - possibly
working in a merchandising or marketing department, or even in a
technical department - who request a transfer to external selling

work on account of the new horizons the job opens up. Examples exist of travellers who began selling work late in their working lives, at up to 50 years of age.[1]

Special features of training

It can thus be seen that the preparation of a commercial traveller for the exercise of his profession is a complex task, requiring a variety of inputs, a considerable proportion of which can be obtained only within the working environment - i.e. after he has been taken into employment - and a highly individualised approach to training.

As a consequence, the training of commercial travellers and representatives is in many countries organised on an in-service basis.

Many large firms, with their own training departments, set up full-scale training courses of their own for their travellers. For instance, in the United States a new entrant to a firm straight out of college, who is destined to join the external sales force, may expect to spend training periods in a number of different departments of the firm employing him, to gain a full understanding of the product (and possibly the production process as well); following this, he may be given instruction in marketing and selling and sent out on one or more tours in the company of an experienced traveller before being sent out on his own. The training process may take as much as two years. The training of a technician already employed in the firm, or of a salesman of low-technology products, will clearly not have to be so comprehensive.

Smaller firms may have recourse to external specialists to run short courses on specific aspects of selling techniques, encourage their employees to attend externally organised courses, or follow the traditional method of sending the newcomer out with an experienced traveller.

Once the traveller is working on his own, the question of follow-up training gives rise to special problems. Since the critical part of his work - the selling interview - cannot normally be carried out under supervision of any kind, he alone can analyse its contents - which approaches were favourably or unfavourably received, what errors he made in presentation, whether failure to close was due to an error on his part or to other circumstances, and so on - and, moreover, is unlikely to have conveniently at hand a supervisor or colleague with whom he can discuss his problems. This isolated situation, in which communications with colleagues are rare, can in certain cases give rise to over-identification with customer attitudes.

---

[1] This ease of entry also attracts considerable numbers of persons who do not fully appreciate the demands which external selling makes on those who practice it. Although no statistics are available on the subject, it is estimated that some 30 per cent of new entrants to the profession leave it within two years.

At a later stage, a need may arise to introduce the traveller to new products or new selling techniques or to prepare him to take on additional tasks such as market research.

One means of dealing with these problems available to the employing firm is the organisation of short courses at the firm's headquarters. All the different techniques used in training courses for other categories of workers can be used here; of particular impact, in view of the importance of interviews with customers, are the training techniques based on role-playing, in which the traveller can act out real-life situations in a low-risk environment and discuss his problems with specialists and with colleagues - a welcome change from the relative isolation in which he usually works. Such courses may also be used to bring salesmen up to date on changes in product, demand or company policies.

In addition to courses organised within the framework of the employing firm, there are in a number of countries courses of a public or private character which travellers and representatives may attend on their own initiative outside working hours. In France, for instance, the National School of Commerce organises one-year sales technician courses, based on evening and Saturday classes, and covering such subjects as the organisation of sales representation work, sales techniques and psychology, financial management, statistics, commercial law, the fundamentals of social labour and fiscal legislation, and human and public relations. In Denmark courses are organised by the Danish Chamber of Manufacturers, the principal commercial travellers' union, various private firms and a special school for export salesmen. In Switzerland there are courses run by public and private institutions (and also by the organisations of travellers themselves) preparing for an examination organised by the professional associations under federal government supervision. Candidates are examined on their knowledge of their respective sectors, sales techniques, organisation and psychology, fundamentals of law, principles of economics, book-keeping, economic geography, the mother tongue and, as an option, a foreign language. Successful candidates are authorised by law to use the title of "certified" representative or agent. Only a few other countries appear to grant an official designation of this kind to travellers and representatives.

A few countries have gone even further with regard to examinations. In Chile there are several full-time post-secondary courses in marketing and sales; but in view of the widespread dissatisfaction expressed by unions as well as employers concerning the standards of some of these courses, the Government is considering the adoption of new legislation to raise standards of training to university level and to create a genuinely professional body of commercial travellers.[1] In Spain, where registration is compulsory, the Colleges of Commercial Agents, which keep the registers of persons entitled to exercise the profession, themselves set examinations for admission.

---

[1] El Mercurio (Santiago de Chile), 31 December 1978.

In addition to formal courses of the kinds described, there are in a number of countries courses specially designed to assist the traveller who is too far away from a training centre to be able to come in regularly to attend evening classes. Correspondence courses have existed for many years; more recently, these have been strengthened with course material recorded on cassettes - or even on videotape, which the traveller on tour can play over on the television set in his hotel room.

While many of these courses are provided without charge, there are apparently some employers who expect their travellers to pay out of their own pockets for any training they do not provide themselves. The tendency in most countries, however, appears to be towards the organisation of training of commercial travellers entirely, or almost entirely, on an in-service basis.

Career development

While in theory commercial travellers and representatives with employee status have the same opportunities for career development as other categories of employees, these opportunities are affected by the special conditions under which their work is performed.

In a large company, with a sales network covering the whole country or a number of countries, career planning is an indispensable tool of manpower planning; and provides a means, not only of ensuring that trained personnel are available to fill line vacancies as they occur, but also of seeing that everybody has a chance to be considered for more responsible jobs. Thus it is possible, for instance, to put field sales personnel through systematic job rotation to determine their abilities. In the field they can be made responsible for new or more complex lines of goods, or transferred to more specialised selling, handling specific types of goods or dealing with special groups of customers. Thus every new salesman is given an opportunity to win by merit promotion to a managerial position, possibly at the highest level. To a lesser extent, career development of this kind is equally possible in small companies. In the career planning programmes which are most effective from the point of view of the traveller as well as that of the company, there is a genuine differentiation of level between the different types of jobs. Certain writers suggest that it is not enough to create pay scales, or a series of job titles, which indicate little more than increases in age or seniority, even if the "promotion" is accompanied by a pay increase; each level of jobs should have its own level of responsibilities, its own level of duties, its own level of requirements in the way of training and experience.[1]

---

[1] On this subect see in particular Thomas F. Stroh: Training and developing the professional salesman (AMACOM, New York, 1973).

However, even in firms with comprehensive training and career planning facilities, career development among travellers and representatives frequently gives rise to problems.

The most important of these is to be found in the nature of external selling work. While, as indicated earlier, the selling of certain types of goods, or negotiations with certain categories of customers, require special knowledge and experience and carry relatively high levels of responsibility, the actual work of a traveller or representative contains very little in terms of line authority. The requirement - which has the force of law in a number of countries - that a traveller must discharge his duties personally precludes recourse to subordinates. This requirement, together with that of full-time employment in external selling, where it exists, means that a traveller who accepts promotion to a supervisory post may have to move partly or entirely out of selling and, in countries where the conditions of entitlement to professional status are strictly defined, lose the status of a traveller and the particular advantages which that status carries.

Each of the travellers employed by a firm is working on his own, usually each with his own area; while some may have more rewarding areas than others, or have a clientele for dealing with which special knowledge or a particularly high degree of responsibility is required, there is little to offer a firm basis for the establishment of a professional hierarchy among travellers and representatives. Even remuneration is not always an accurate guide to standing; a traveller selling repeat consumer or industrial goods in an area in which he has built up a good clientele may earn more than one selling complex machinery each sale of which requires protracted negotiations demanding a high level of technical and background knowledge from the salesman - and even, in certain cases, more than his own sales manager.

Similarly, a traveller who changes his employer may benefit in terms of pay or fringe benefits, job satisfaction or other considerations; but he will remain a traveller; no upgrading is likely to derive from the move.

This flatness in the structure of the profession, and the fact that promotion frequently involves a radical change in status and job content, has meant that travellers and representatives do not always find the prospects of promotion entirely to their taste. A traveller may, for instance, be reluctant to move into an office job, where his freedom of action is relatively circumscribed and he has fewer opportunities for travelling and meeting people outside his firm. In addition, if he is earning substantial commissions in an area in which he has built up a large clientele, a transfer to an office post on fixed salary - even where it carries a promotion - may result in a substantial loss of income for him. In fact, one major problem of management is that of devising pay schemes which will avoid, on the one hand, situations arising where a traveller will be deterred from accepting a transfer to the headquarters staff by financial considerations and, on the other hand, those where a good traveller is tempted to find sales employment elsewhere by the lure of higher earnings prospects.

In some countries in which the legal status of travellers and
representatives is not strictly defined, individual firms have overcome the problem to some extent by introducing various forms of
team sales, in which the team leader receives "override" commissions
on all sales by members of the team.

A representative with more than one employer is likely to
have special problems of career development. Although he has
employee status in the eyes of the law, his relationships with the
occupational hierarchies in the firms employing him are liable to
be tenuous. He may have a greater incentive to seek income
security than a traveller who is in the employ of one firm only;
but where an opportunity for promotion presents itself in one of the
firms employing him, he is likely to find himself, in his isolated
position, at a disadvantage in comparison with travellers employed
full-time by that firm. If he does succeed in obtaining a full-
time post he will have to give up his other representation contracts and may suffer financial prejudice as a result.

Thus for many travellers and representatives, career development may be confined to the development of the clientele in the
areas they cover - of getting to know the wants of "their" customers
and how best to meet them and of building up relations of trust
which will keep the customers faithful. This can be a source of
considerable personal satisfaction and ensure steadily rising
earnings; but it is not the same as career development within the
hierarchy of an employing firm.

For many travellers, in fact, there eventually comes a time of
choice - to move up the sales hierarchy of the firms employing them,
but to give up their chosen profession (although they are likely to
participate in the development of sales techniques and in the training of other salesmen); or to remain in their profession, refusing
all opprtunities of line promotion, and concentrate on the development of their clientele - in the same way as a commercial agent
does. For the most ambitious and entrepreneurial, in fact, there
may be an alternative course - to set up commercial agencies of
their own.

CHAPTER IV

THE EXERCISE OF THE PROFESSION

This chapter discusses successively the special forms which
the obligations incumbent on employees generally take on for
commercial travellers and representatives and some of the special
problems which arise in connection with their conditions of work
and employment. Questions of pay and expenses are examined in
Chapters V and VI.

The general obligations of the employee
as applicable to commercial
travellers and representatives

Where an external salesman has employee status, he is subject
to the general obligations incumbent on all employees, namely to
perform his work personally, conscientiously and diligently; to
comply faithfully with the employer's instructions in the performance of his work, and in particular to adhere to the employer's
conditions of sale; to safeguard the interests of his employer
(including his business secrets) and to refrain from any act prejudicial to those interests; and to treat with reasonable care
the material provided by the employer for the performance of his
work.

However, the position of a traveller or representative
vis-à-vis his employer is an unusual one. He does not normally
(unless he is a local agent) work from the offices of his employer
or call there regularly to receive instructions: he may live a
considerable distance away, and go there only for special reasons.
He is thus not subject to physical supervision in the same way
as employees working in a factory or an office. Travellers'
contracts sometimes state that the traveller must accept supervision as necessary (e.g. a visit from a district sales manager
or inspector); but in normal circumstances such supervision will
be occasional. He may also receive instructions to visit a
customer urgently, and some firms send their travellers detailed
schedules of visits to be made; but frequently the traveller
has considerable latitude - especially as regards actual interviewing - to plan his own work and use his own judgement in line
with company policy. A representative, acting for several firms,
may enjoy even more freedom than a traveller in this regard.
This is, in fact, one of the features of external sales work which
travellers and representatives find most attractive.[1]

The position of the traveller or representative, and in
particular this freedom of action, affects the manner in which
these obligations apply to him.

---

[1] See, for instance, the results of the inquiry into the
profession published in Promouvoir (Brussels, Centrale nationale
des employés), No. 27, special issue, June 1971.

Compliance with employer's instructions

As has already been mentioned, the instructions given by the employer concerning the work of a traveller or representative may be of an extremely general character, merely requiring the traveller or representative to use his best efforts to obtain orders in a prescribed area.   This general instruction may be backed up by training in the organisation of sales work, in the setting of priorities and in route planning on the basis of customer potential.   At the other extreme, a company seeking to keep its external sales force under tight control may provide its travellers with detailed daily schedules of calls.

The instructions issued by the employer are likely also to cover the question of reporting on activities.   The great majority of travellers and representatives are required to submit daily reports; but the frequency may be less.   The subject-matter of the reports includes, naturally, orders obtained during the reference period; but travellers may also be required to report on the state of the market in the area, customer reactions, customers' financial standing and the activities of competitors.

It is clearly in the employer's interest to be kept informed of market developments; but inasmuch as reports have to be prepared outside working hours, or their preparation keeps the traveller away from selling work (especially if his earnings are entirely, or to a substantial extent, made up of commission), excessive reporting requirements are likely to be resented by him.

A further problem arises with regard to observance of the employer's conditions of sale.   A traveller or representative seeking to gain a new customer or to keep an existing one may find himself under considerable pressure, in the course of a selling interview, to offer concessions and have to take an immediate decision; in such cases he is expected to make any concessions he offers subject to acceptance by his employer.   Some firms in the United States, however, allow their salesmen to negotiate from a float of manufacturing cost if this is necessary to meet a competitor's price.

This requirement has legal backing in a number of countries. In the legislation defining commercial travellers and their functions, reference is frequently made to the right of the employer to accept or refuse an order obtained by his field sales-man (frequently in connection with entitlement to commission).

In practically all cases - except where the employer has specifically given his salesman powers to conclude contracts binding on him - an order taken is subject to acceptance, explicit or tacit, by the employer.   This provision, while in most cases only of formal significance, reflects the special position of the external salesman.   For instance, having only a fragmentary view of the over-all sales position of his employer, he is not always in a position to give firm delivery dates.   In addition, it gives the employer certain safeguards; for instance, he may have grounds for belief that the customer will be unable to pay for the goods ordered, or a concession made may run counter to his general sales policy.   For reasons such as these, it is understandable that the employer should wish to reserve the right to accept an order with reservations or to decline it.   However, where an employer does

refuse an order, he is required under the law of some countries
(Belgium, Uruguay) to inform the traveller of his reasons for doing
so; sometimes, too, the law fixes a time-limit for rejection of
an order (Argentina, Belgium, Brazil) or states that the order shall
be deemed to be accepted unless the employer refuses it without
delay (Austria).

In a number of countries the legislation on commercial
travellers also covers persons with the right to conclude transactions binding on the employer within the definition of employee
travellers and representatives. As a safeguard for the customer,
the law sometimes provides that authorisation to that effect
must be given in writing. The safeguards regarding compliance
with the employer's conditions of sale applies particularly to
such cases; Swiss law expressly provides that the traveller or
representative must reserve the right of the employer to refuse
any change proposed.

In certain cases a traveller or representative may also be
required or authorised by his employer to collect moneys due or to
modify terms of payment. This power would seem to apply either
where the traveller is empowered to conclude transactions binding
on his employer (in which case he might receive an initial payment
on account) or after delivery of the goods.

These powers appear to date back to times when communications
and credit transfer systems were less highly developed than today;
but their usefulness has diminished over the years. Thus, in
Switzerland, they have now been circumscribed by amendments to
the relevant legislation which came into force in 1972, and
special authorisation from the employer is now required in that
country to collect moneys due or offer special terms of payment.
In introducing the new legislation the competent authorities
were actually seeking to promote among customers a premise that
the traveller's function is confined to the taking of orders, and
that they should require from the traveller proof of authorisation
to receive moneys before making any payment.[1] Denmark has
similar legislation; there the Commissions Act forbids external
salesmen to accept payments, grant price concessions or offer
special terms of payment.

Nevertheless, the collection, by the traveller or representative, of moneys due still appears to be an accepted practice in a
number of countries. In Argentina under the law, in New South
Wales under the state wage award, and in Italy under collective
agreements, a traveller collecting moneys due as a subsidiary
part of his duties is entitled to additional payment. In the
Federation of Malaysia, however, the collection of moneys due
appears to be frequently an obligation for the traveller; it is
even reported that the rate of commission (which is in any case
not payable until the customer has paid) is reduced where the
customer is tardy in paying. This obligation lays on the
traveller a heavy burden of responsibility for the successful
outcome of the transaction.

---

[1] "Message du Conseil fédéral à l'Assemblée fédérale concernant la révision des titres dixième et dixième bis du code des
obligations", in Feuille fédérale (Berne), 119th year, Vol. II,
No. 40, 5 Oct. 1967, pp. 421-422.

A traveller or representative may also be called upon to conduct market research, participate in sales campaigns, help customers to prepare and set up display material, attend trade fairs and make suggestions for possible changes in the presentation or design of goods sold. Again, these tasks, while necessary from the employer's standpoint, may be resented by travellers for the same reasons as the reporting requirement, particularly where no additional payment is made. However, in several wage awards in Australia (which provide for a guaranteed minimum of weekly earnings, even where the traveller is on commission only), there is provision that special payments shall be made in respect of attendance at trade fairs, exhibitions or agricultural shows after 6 p.m. Mondays to Fridays inclusive. In New Zealand, travellers may to some extent be relieved of the requirement to perform display work by the creation, under the national wage award, of a special category of "Display travellers" wholly or substantially engaged in establishing or installing displays of their employers' products.

Safeguarding the employer's interests

The exposure of commercial travellers and representatives to outside contacts, and the continual need to form independent judgements on the basis of the facts locally available, lay special responsibilities on them with regard to the protection of their employers' interests.

One consideration which a traveller or representative has to bear continually in mind is that of ensuring that the business he obtains is good business for his employer - and, in particular, that the customer is able to pay for the goods he orders. He is thus sometimes expected by his employer to make inquiries into the financial standing of customers and prospects and to report back on the subject where necessary. Information of this kind may in many cases be useful to an employer when deciding whether or not to accept an order; but there are equally certainly cases in which a commercial investigation agency will be able to provide the employer with a much more comprehensive view of a customer's credit worthiness than that which a traveller can build up on such information as he gleans in the course of his selling activities.

Another area in which a traveller or representative has special responsibilities is that of the protection of his employer's business secrets, in so far as they are known to him.

The very fact that a traveller or representative, by the nature of his work, is in continual contact with persons outside the employer's establishment - primarily customers, but possibly representatives of competing firms as well - imposes on him an obligation of special caution regarding the interests of his employer or employers greatly exceeding that of employees whose work is performed largely on the employer's premises.

All travellers and representatives are concerned by the obligation to safeguard their employers' business secrets. These may be either of a technical character - relating to the manufacturing processes and the methods of organising production used by the employer - or of a commercial or financial character, relating to such matters as sales organisation, clientele, pricing policies, supply sources, etc.

Except where sales of high-technology goods are involved, a traveller will not generally require an extensive knowledge of his employer's manufacturing processes for the purpose of his work. On the other hand, he is likely to possess information on the commercial side of his employer's business which the employer may wish to keep confidential.

While the law in most countries does not generally impose on commercial travellers and representatives any obligations to secrecy going beyond those applicable to employees in general, individual contracts of employment frequently include special clauses on the subject.

Another field in which special caution is necessary is the avoidance of situations in which a traveller or representative may cause his employer actual prejudice by diverting elsewhere business which would in normal circumstances have gone to him.

Such situations are particularly likely to arise, in the absence of safeguards, where a sales representative is working for more than one employer - a practice authorised, implicitly or explicitly, by the legislation of a number of countries.

In most occupations the nature of the work is such as to re- quire the complete attention and physical presence of the worker while he is performing it; thus even where a worker is allowed to work for a second employer,[1] he is physically debarred from doing more than one job at a time. In contrast, a sales representative working for several employers will frequently find himself in a position where he is offering a customer the goods of more than one of his employers (and thus, in a sense, working for more than one of them) simultaneously, and problems of conflict of interest could easily arise if one of the items offered were at all similar to another.

For this reason, where the right to work for more than one employer is recognised in principle, it is qualified in various ways, usually designed to avoid such conflicts of interest, and prejudice to an employer, arising therefrom.

Thus under the legislation in force in the Federal Republic of Germany and Switzerland a traveller may not undertake transac- tions for other firms without the employer's consent. In France, the legislation in force states that a contract of employ- ment may contain a prohibition on the offer for sale of specific types of goods, or the goods of specific firms; in the absence of any such prohibition the contract must contain a list of the firms or goods the representative already deals with and an undertaking not to take on additional business without the employer's consent (or a specific waiver of the application of that rule). Where there is more than one employer, the consent of all must be obtained. Similar provisions are to be found in model contracts in use in a number of countries. In the discussions between the organisations of representatives and employers during the preparation of the draft EEC directive concerning commercial trav- ellers and representatives, a majority consensus appears to have emerged on both sides concerning the need for the requirement of prior authorisation.

---

[1] In Denmark, for instance, under section 15 of the Employers and Salaried Employees (Legal Relationships) Act, a salaried employee has the right to undertake duties outside his employment without the employer's consent, provided the duties can be discharged without inconvenience to the enterprise.

These regulations are similar in content to those applicable
to commercial agents in similar circumstances.   A few countries,
however, have dealt with the problem in a more radical fashion.
Thus, in Sweden a traveller is not entitled to employee status if
he sells goods for more than one firm.   The situation appears
to be similar in the Federation of Malaysia, the Netherlands and
the United Kingdom.   In South Australia travellers working for
more than one employer are excluded from the scope of the commercial travellers' award.

A similar prohibition is found in some countries on the
conduct by a traveller or representative of business for his own
account without the employer's permission.   In some countries,
where the definition of the commercial traveller states that
business is sought "for the account of one or more firms", the
prohibition is implied;   in others (Austria, France, the Federal
Republic of Germany) it is more explicit.   Sometimes, too,
penalties are laid down: in France a traveller or representative
doing business for his own account is liable to exclusion from the
benefit of the special legislation on travellers and representatives;
in Austria the employer may require that a transaction concluded
for the traveller's account be transferred to his account or,
alternatively, claim damages.

Working on own account may, of course, raise questions regarding the right of the traveller or representative concerned to
employee status in addition to giving rise to a risk of unfair
competition.

Protection of material provided by the employer

The employer's general obligation to provide his employee
with all the items necessary for the performance of his work is
met, in the case of a traveller or representative, by the provision
of information on the goods to be offered for sale, prices, delivery
times and other subjects on which the traveller needs to be informed;
he may also provide a car.   In addition, he provides him with
samples of the goods to be offered.   These documents and samples
are the principal "tools" of a traveller's trade.

Samples remain the property of the employer, and must normally
be returned to him on demand or on the expiry of the employment
relationship.   However, this does not seem to have been always the
case;   evidence of this can be found, for instance, in the national
collective agreement for travellers and representatives in force in
France, which contains a clause providing that an employer may not
require a traveller to purchase the samples entrusted to him.

The traveller has the custody of the samples with which the
employer has provided him and is responsible for keeping them in
good condition and protecting them against loss, damage or destruction.   Where the samples are of value, this can be a heavy
responsibility.

Cases exist where employers have required travellers to pay
deposits covering the value of the samples entrusted to them.
To prevent possible abuses, the law in France and Belgium, and the
collective agreements in force in Italy, provide that any deposits
paid in by a traveller shall be held, not by the employer, but
by an authorised bank or other institution.   The collective agreements in force in Italy contain a further restriction: a deposit
may only be required where the value of the samples is such as
to justify it.   The tendency, however, appears to be towards the
replacement of deposits by insurance policies taken out by employers.   Lastly, in Australia (New South Wales) the current award
relieves the traveller of all financial liability in respect
of loss, theft or destruction of the samples entrusted to him,
provided he can prove the absence of fraud or negligence on his
part.

Conditions of work and employment:
special aspects

Administrative controls

In several countries all commercial travellers and representatives are required by law to be officially registered as such,
and unregistered persons practising the profession - as well as
persons employing them - are liable to penalties.

The principal reason for this requirement, where it exists,
appears to be the protection of the public, and in particular the
prevention of abuses by persons passing themselves off as
travellers or representatives.   Confirmation of this thesis is
to be found in the fact that registration frequently gives rise
to the issue of a professional identity document, sometimes
bearing the name of the employer or specifying the nature of
the goods sold (thus providing proof of a relationship with the
firm whose goods are offered) and issued by an administrative
authority (not the employer himself).   Further confirmation is
to be found in the fact that any unregistered person who practises
the profession, and any person employing an unregistered traveller
or representative, are liable to penalties.   Arrangements of this
kind exist in, for instance, Austria, Chile, Colombia, Ecuador,
France, Peru, Spain, Switzerland[1] and Tunisia.   However, a number
of other countries, including the Benelux countries, the Federal
Republic of Germany, Italy, the United Kingdom and the United
States, have no such regulation.

To obtain registration a traveller or representative must
produce, in addition to proof of identity, proof that he is
actually employed as a traveller or representative; this usually
takes the form of certificates of employment from the firm or
firms employing him. He may also be required to produce evidence
of good behaviour; this may take the form of a copy of the
applicant's police record (in countries where production of these
can be required) or, alternatively, certificates of good conduct
issued by persons of standing in the applicant's place of residence.   Evidence of a recent conviction in respect of a serious
offence, or an offence involving dishonesty, is generally considered
as sufficient grounds for rejecting the application.

---

[1] In Switzerland self-employed commercial agents are subject
to the same registration requirements as employee commercial
travellers.

The identity document, once issued, is usually valid for a limited period only (e.g. one year). On the occasion of each renewal, new proof of employment as a traveller or representative is required, and any changes in the firm or firms represented are recorded. On cessation of activity within the profession - even temporarily - the document is generally withdrawn.

In the majority of the countries in which arrangements of this kind do exist, their primary purpose appears to be the provision to the traveller by a public authority of proof of his calling for presentation to third parties, combined with an initial verification of his past record. In a few, however, registration entails admission to a formal professional register, kept by a body with responsibilities for upholding standards of professional conduct.

In Uruguay, for instance, registration is administered by the National Labour Institute, which is assisted by an advisory board of five members, two of whom are appointed by the Chambers of Commerce and Industry and two by the Federation of Commercial Agents. This board makes recommendations on applications for registration and hears complaints against individual travellers and representatives in respect of alleged breaches of the law, professional misconduct and acts of such a nature as to bring the profession into discredit; it also keeps records of all contracts of employment of travellers and representatives and advises on ways and means of applying the relevant legislation, with particular reference to prevention of the illegal practice of the profession.

In Spain responsibility for registration is in the hands of the Professional Colleges of Commercial Agents, public-law corporations responsible for the representation, co-ordination and defence of the interests of their members. They have wide powers with regard to registration. They set minimum educational requirements for admission, conduct entrance examinations, award diplomas to successful candidates and investigate their past records, issue and renew professional identity documents, levy entrance and membership fees, uphold standards of professional conduct (and impose fines for breaches of professional ethics) and combat the clandestine practice of the profession, if necessary by legal action against the persons concerned and those employing them. They may even set up inspection services to seek out cases of such activity.

The contract of employment

The great majority of commercial travellers and representatives work under individual contracts of employment.

The content of each contract is affected by a variety of considerations peculiar to the profession, such as the type of goods or services sold, the area or clientele to be covered, the composition of remuneration (salary, commission, bonuses), expense payment arrangements, admission to the company's employee benefit schemes, non-disclosure of business secrets, periods of notice and non-competition clauses. The treatment of each of these factors varies according to the policy of the firm concerned.

In the great majority of cases the contract of employment of a commercial traveller or representative is an individual agreement concluded between him and his employer. Both employers' organisations and trade unions offer their members advice on how to deal with the main items a contract should cover and make available model contracts; but their role is purely advisory, and in many cases their advice may not even be sought by the parties.

Contracts once signed "stand as the law as between those who have made them", as section 1134 of the French Civil Code puts it, and may not be revoked save with the consent of the parties or for reasons authorised by law. This principle applies, in its essentials at any rate, in contracts of employment. However, one of the basic assumptions underlying contract law generally is that of the equality of the contracting parties; but in the relationships between an employer and a prospective employee this equality does not in practice exist.[1] The very fact that the employer has it in his power to give out, or to withhold, the subject-matter of the contract - the job - tips the balance of bargaining power decisively in his favour.

In some countries measures have been taken to redress the balance to some extent. Certain possible abuses (to which reference is made elsewhere in this chapter) may be forbidden by law, while in a few countries, minimum conditions of employment are laid down by binding awards. Similarly, in countries in which travellers and representatives are unionised and covered by collective agreements, the support of the unions concerned improves their bargaining strength. However, measures of this kind have not been taken in all countries; and, as has been seen, where unions do exist, many travellers and representatives do not join them.

The foregoing gives an indication of the importance of the individual contract of employment in the determination of the conditions of employment of commercial travellers and representatives.

The law applicable to the employment of travellers and representatives frequently contains little or no guidance regarding the form and content of their contracts of employment; this question is left for the parties to decide. There are, however, some exceptions to this general rule. The law in Chile, Switzerland, Tunisia and Uruguay requires that their contracts of employment be in writing. The Swiss Code of Obligations states in addition that the contract (which may not take the form of a letter of appointment) must stipulate, inter alia, its duration and date of expiry; the powers of the traveller; remuneration and expenses; and, where one of the parties if resident outside Switzerland, the national law applicable. In the absence of a written contract, the courts are required to settle disputes by reference to established practice in the sector concerned rather than to any statements by the parties on verbal understandings.

---

[1] "The individual employee or worker has normally no social power, because it is only in the most exceptional cases that as an individual he has any bargaining power at all ... typically, the worker as an individual has to accept the conditions which the employer offers" (O. Kahn-Freund: Labour and the law (London, Stevens, 1977, p.6).

In Uruguay the law lays down even more detailed requirements; the contracts of travellers and representatives must state details of remuneration (and the method of remuneration) and expenses; whether the traveller is empowered to collect moneys due; the area or clientele assigned to him; and whether or not he is allowed to act for other firms or is responsible for the physical delivery of goods ordered.

In the majority of countries, however, the requirement of a written contract does not appear to exist in law.[1]

Hence the contracts under which travellers and representatives are employed vary widely in form and content. At one extreme there is the detailed written document covering a wide range of questions, including the purpose of the contract (types of goods to be sold), professional status, membership of the general and complementary social security schemes, probation, the area assigned and procedures for changing it, the right to represent other firms, pay, methods of payment and expenses, methods of calculating and paying commission, orders on which commission is due, reporting requirements, professional secrecy, the use of a company car, samples, termination, goodwill indemnities and the radius clause.[2] At the other extreme there is the letter of appointment - which may be little more than a communication of a decision by the employer to take a traveller into his service and contain little or nothing regarding terms and conditions of employment - or a vague verbal understanding which leaves the traveller dependent on the employer's goodwill.

In the absence of a written document clearly setting out terms and conditions of employment and agreed to by the parties, the traveller has little protection against the unilateral imposition by the employer of changes in conditions of service (possibly to his disadvantage); and in the event of a dispute which goes to the courts, the task of the latter is frequently complicated by the lack of that information concerning the intentions of the parties which a written contract can provide.

The traveller and his territory

As mentioned earlier, many travellers and representatives are allocated territories or lists of customers in respect of which they alone represent their employers. In some countries, such as France, the law actually requires that a traveller's contract must specify the geographical area or clientele allotted to him.

---

[1] Mention may, however, be made of the requirement, under the national collective agreements in force in Italy, that the employer must give each traveller a letter of appointment stating the duration of the probationary period, the area of operation, the traveller's powers, non-selling duties, minimum travelling time and pay.

[2] Model contract drawn up by the French Union of Metallurgical and Mining Industries (UIMM) in 1970; see UIMM: Les représentants de commerce (Paris, 1970), pp. 182-184.

The assignment of an area or clientele to a traveller or representative is an important feature of the profession.   It gives him a group of customers or prospects whose needs he can get to know well and with whom he can develop relations of trust and goodwill, thereby ensuring a steady flow of orders; at the same time, it gives him protection against poaching by colleagues seeking to improve their own sales figures.   Thus the transfer of a traveller from one territory or area to another, or a change in the size of his territory or clientele, can give rise to special problems where the system of remuneration in use contains a significant incentive element.

There are circumstances - for instance, where business has fallen off in a territory;   where new territories are to be opened up - where it is in the interest of the employer to move a traveller from one territory to another. However, such a decision can in certain circumstances cause considerable prejudice to the traveller concerned.   He may have been in his territory for some years and have built up a large and well-established clientele from whose orders he derives substantial amounts of commission. In such circumstances a transfer to a new area in which the clientele has to be built up - which in a sense is a mark of confidence in him on the part of the employer - can, paradoxically, lead to a substantial loss of earnings until the clientele in the new area has been rebuilt.

A similar situation can arise where the employer decides to modify the boundaries of a traveller's territory or area - for instance, dividing it into two and putting a second traveller in one half, possibly on the grounds that he considers it too large to be adequately covered by one person.

A representative working for several firms is less liable to transfer than a traveller working for one firm;   but he is subject to boundary changes in the same way.

In a few countries the law or collective agreements provide the traveller with some protection against the possibility of financial prejudice resulting from such changes.   Thus the collective agreements for commercial travellers in Italy and the relevant legislation in Argentina and Mexico provide that where a traveller is transferred, he must receive in the new area the same earnings as before (in Argentina the rule applies also when a territory or clientele is reduced), while in Switzerland a traveller whose territory or clientele is modified can claim compensation if he wishes and may in addition terminate the contract with just cause.   In several countries provision is made requiring payment of travel and removal expenses for the traveller and his family;   in Italy a traveller whose transfer causes him to terminate the lease on his residence prematurely must also be given the amount of compensation he has to pay to the landlord, subject to a maximum of six months' earnings.   In Australia (New South Wales), however, the award in force merely provides that an employer may not reduce or alter a territory to the detriment of the traveller save after giving three months' written notice of his intention, while in Denmark no provision for compensation exists.

In some cases the right of the employer to transfer a traveller to another area for valid operational reasons is specifically recognised by law; but in Mexico and Panama no transfer may be made without the traveller's consent, while in France the courts have ruled that a traveller may legitimately refuse a change in the size of his sector if he fears a resultant loss of earnings, unless the change is dictated by operational necessity.[1]

One special case deserves mention. A transfer may cause a traveller to leave an area in which he has lived for a number of years and in which he and his family have established roots. If the contract of employment is terminated soon after the transfer, he may find himself stranded in a strange town and thus have more difficulty in obtaining new employment than he would if he had not moved. This contingency has been provided for in South Australia, where the relevant wage award provides that if, within the two years following the change of residence, employment is terminated through no fault of the employee and the employee decides to return to his home town within a period of 90 days, travel and removal expenses for himself and his family must be paid to him by the employer.

In France, under a special agreement dated 22 June 1970, the reduction of a salesman's territory or clientele is permissible only to safeguard him from termination on grounds of redundancy. If the salesman accepts a proposal to reduce his territory in such circumstances he is guaranteed, for a period equivalent to the period of notice of termination to which he would have been entitled, monthly earnings equivalent to his average monthly earnings over the 12 months preceding the reduction of his territory or clientele and, in certain circumstances, 70 per cent of those earnings during a subsequent period of 3 months.

Hours of work

The hours of work of commercial travellers and representatives cannot be measured in the same way as those of most other groups of employees.

For most manual workers, as well as for shop and office employ- ees, hours of work are roughly equivalent to hours of attendance at the place of work; there is some kind of recording system; and the nature of the work being done is known.

For a commercial traveller, the situation is different. First, working hours are determined by factors which are substan- tially outside the traveller's control - travelling time, railway timetables, waiting time, the amount of time needed to close a sale with an individual customer, etc. - and by his own personal motivation. Secondly, they include substantial amounts of non- selling work - preparation of interviews, updating of customer records, reports to his employer, and above all travelling and waiting (an element which has been estimated as taking up, in extreme cases, as much as 50 per cent of a traveller's working

---

[1] Union des industries métallurgiques et minières: Travail et main d'oeuvre, 13th edition, Vol. 1, p. 1065.

time.[1]   Travelling, from the point of view of the traveller, is
a relatively unproductive part of working hours;   either he has
to organise his journeys outside the normal working day (which is
sometimes difficult, if not impossible) or he has to accept the
fact that part of the normal working day will be unproductive
and catch up when the normal working day is over.   Hence the
traveller may have to write his reports and prepare his interviews
after working hours in a hotel room;   or during weekends at his
home.   He is, as regards hours of work, on a par with the
professional worker: he goes on working until what has to be done
has been done, regardless of the time it takes him.   At the same
time, his personal motivation can affect his working hours of work,
especially if there is a substantial incentive component in his
pay;   one traveller may strain unceasingly to sell all he can,
while another may be reluctant to make the effort to sell more
than he needs to sell to ensure himself a reasonable living.
Lastly, on account of the continual absence of travellers from
the employer's place of business, their hours of work are difficult
to supervise.

It is possibly because of the difficulty of establishing any
generally acceptable standard of hours of work for commercial
travellers and representatives that they are in a number of
countries specifically excluded from the scope of the legislation
on hours of work.   This is the case in Belgium, the Netherlands,
Norway, Brazil, Luxembourg, Chile, and Denmark;   while in Sweden
the legislation on hours of work does not apply where the employer
is unable to exercise effective supervision of working hours.   In
other countries, such as Austria, France and the Federal Republic
of Germany and Spain, the law is silent on the subject.

In several countries, however, the granting of employee status
to travellers and representatives has brought them within the
scope of the general legislation on hours of work or that applicable to the hours of work of salaried employees.   This is the
case in Argentina, Brazil, Egypt, Ecuador, Finland and Panama;
but Panama excludes travellers working for more than one employer
from the scope of hours-of-work legislation.   In New Zealand the
commercial travellers' award limits their working hours to an
average of 40 per week.   In Mexico the official working week for
travellers is 40 hours, as for other workers;   any checks needed
on hours actually worked are made on the basis of travellers'
reports.   However, the authorities in several of the countries
in which the hours of work legislation is applicable recognise
that its enforcement is difficult as far as commercial travellers
are concerned.

In addition, the general provisions concerning working hours
in some collective agreements are applicable to commercial
travellers.

---

[1] R.C. Smyth and M.J. Murphy: _Compensating and Motivating
Salesmen_ (American Management Association, 1969), pp. 89-90.   It
has been estimated that, on the average, only 20-33 per cent of a
traveller's time is spent in actual conversation with customers
(Stroh, op. cit. p. 171).

In the United Kingdom, where no provisions of a general character applicable to commercial travellers and representatives appear to exist, their biggest union has taken the position that although fixed hours of work are not necessarily relevant to the employment of commercial representatives, such hours of work as may be agreed in negotiating contracts of employment shall include provision for any administrative duties within the job specification concerned.

Where the duration of the working week is fixed by law or collective agreement, there is a theoretical possibility that a traveller whose actual working hours exceed the statutory maximum can claim overtime payment. However, the possibility appears to be little more than theoretical, since overtime is generally paid for only if carried out on the express instructions of the employer. Sometimes there is a specific exclusion: one model contract in use in the United Kingdom, while setting normal hours of work, expressly states that no overtime will be paid if owing to the exigencies of the work the normal hours are exceeded, while the general collective agreement for the food and drink industry in Hamburg-Schleswig-Hostein (Federal Republic of Germany) states that an employee receiving travel expenses is not entitled to overtime pay.

On the other hand, in Australia (New South Wales) overtime rates are payable for selling work done on public holidays. In the Federal Republic of Germany, the general collective agreement for North Rhine-Westphalia provides for specially negotiated compensation for overtime; but any such compensation paid is not to be considered as overtime pay. The collective agreement for the wholesale and retail trades in another province (Hesse) in the same country sets a financial qualification; it states that a traveller on fixed salary and commission is covered by the clauses on overtime only if his total monthly earnings do not exceed 115 per cent of the monthly wage set in the collective agreement for the category to which he belongs.

Weekly rest

In the earlier years of the profession, when communications were slow, weekly rest could be a serious problem; a traveller might be away from home for several weeks, or even months, at a time. However, with the improvements which have taken place in transport facilities and in the status of travellers, weekly rest has become less of a problem. As one study made in the United States[1] puts it:

> The days of weary Willie Loman[2] hitting the road with his sample case on a three-month train trip from town to town are over. ... Willie and his contemporaries ... staying in dreary rooming houses or cheap hotels and living off the "swindle sheet", they had very little normal home life ... Today's typical salesman ... ordinarily he is away from home only a few nights a week.

While the general situation has improved considerably, there are still many salesmen (especially those selling in foreign countries) who may have to spend weeks, and even months, at a time away from home, and for whom weekly rest remains a problem.

---

[1] Smyth and Murphy, op. cit., pp. 11-12.

[2] The hero of Arthur Miller's Death of a Salesman.

In a number of countries, where travellers and representatives have won employee status, they have at the same time gained entitlement to weekly rest.   Sometimes this entitlement is spelt out in the legislation concerning the profession: in other cases it is acquired as an implicit consequence of their designation as employees.   Exclusions of travellers and representatives from the scope of the legislation on weekly rest appear to be less frequent than exclusions from that on working hours.

Where the entitlement exists, it is frequently applied in a flexible fashion.   Thus, for instance, in Panama a traveller is entitled on his return home to one day of rest for every 7 days' travelling time, this over and above the weekly rest to which he is entitled under general legislation.   In Argentina a similar provision is in force, providing for additional 36 hours' rest for every week of travelling.   In Western Australia a traveller is entitled to an extra day's annual leave for every four weekends during which he is absent from his house or his employer's business.   In Italy the national collective agreements for commercial travellers provide that where a traveller is unable to return home for over a month he is entitled to compensatory leave corresponding to the number of days of weekly rest not taken and to travel expenses home and back.   They also provide that the working week may consist of five full days or four full days and two half days, and that in branches of activity with seasonal peaks a six-day week may be worked in peak periods and compensated by a four-day week during slack periods.   In Switzerland there are no provisions on the subject either in law or in collective agreements; but in practice travellers and representatives usually have Sunday and one other day off each week.

In this field, too, the regulations are difficult to enforce, since there is no practicable means of preventing a traveller from, for example, preparing his reports or updating his records on his rest day.

Holidays with pay

A major advantage enjoyed by commercial travellers and representatives with employee status, as compared with persons doing similar work but on a self-employed basis, is the statutory entitlement to holidays with pay.

In all countries where holidays with pay are an accepted practice, travellers and representatives with employee status appear to enjoy this right in the same way as other groups of workers: a minimum is usually laid down in the relevant legislation, which is frequently improved upon in collective agreements or, in the case of commercial travellers and representatives, individual contracts of employment.   However, additional holidays sometimes granted under collective agreements on the basis of age or seniority are not always granted to commercial travellers and representatives.[1]

Some special problems arise in connection with the provision of holidays with pay for travellers and representatives.

One problem, affecting only representatives with more than one employer, is that of fixing a period for the holiday, since all the employers must give their agreement.   To the extent that the representative has considerable freedom in the fixing of his travel

---

[1] Union des industries métallurgiques et minières, op. cit., p. 537.

schedules, the problem may not be a serious one; but if one or more employers have laid down strict work requirements, agreement may prove difficult.

A more important and complex problem is the calculation of the amount of pay due in respect of the holiday.   The general rule is that a worker shall receive at least the remuneration he would normally have earned if he had worked during the holiday period.   However, many travellers and representatives have a substantial incentive element in their earnings (and considerable numbers are paid entirely by results); moreover, as is seen elsewhere, the amount of the incentive element can vary greatly from one pay period to another.

Consequently, the usual method used to calculate holiday pay in such cases is to take average earnings (fixed salary plus commission) over a period immediately preceding the holiday and to calculate the amount of pay due on a pro rata basis.   The length of the reference period is usually twelve months; but in certain countries it is less (six months, or even three).   Where the fixed salary or commission paid includes an amount to cover expenses, that amount is deducted from the total thus calculated - not unreasonably, since the traveller will not be working and will consequently not incur expenses.   However, the amount of any previous holiday pay during the reference period is sometimes included, thus making a reference basis consisting of a full year's earnings.   In addition, the traveller will continue during the holiday period to accumulate commission on orders obtained by him before his departure.   On the other hand, where he is entitled to commission on orders received directly by the employer from customers in this area, the entitlement may lapse during the holiday period.

No specific rules conerning holiday pay for salesmen with more than one employer have been encountered; but if one assumes the application to them of the general principle - in force in such countries as Argentina, Australia (Victoria), Brazil, Chile and France - namely that for an employee with variable earnings the holiday pay shall be calculated on the basis of average earnings over a set period immediately preceding the holiday - it would seem that each employer should contribute on the basis of the remuneration actually paid by him.

A special problem arises for travellers and representatives paid mainly or entirely by commission in connection with public holidays, during which they cannot visit customers and consequently cannot earn commission.   The International Federation of Commercial, Clerical and Technical Employees (FIET) has recommended, in its World Action Programme adopted in 1976, that travellers and representatives should receive an allowance for public holidays.

Health

Although little or nothing is available in the way of studies and statistics on the subject, the view is widely held that the practice of the profession of commercial traveller or representative demands a high standard of physical and psychic health.   The hours of work, the continual travelling and changes of lodging, the constant pressure to achieve results, the importance of being at a peak of "form" for each important interview so as to give the most favourable projection of his employer's image as well as his own, and other factors combine to place an external salesman under continual strain.

While there do not appear to be any occupational diseases
officially attributed to the exercise of the profession, there
are several factors which are recognised as likely to promote
certain types of disorders and as having a generally deleterious
effect on travellers' health.

The most widely recognised factor is that of driving.   The
incidence of this factor varies considerably: a local agent may
do all his travelling within the boundaries of a single town,
whereas a traveller with a large area to cover may spend three
or four hours at the wheel of his care every day.   It is stated
that continual driving tends to give rise to disorders such as
spinal disorders (among others, slipped discs), osteoarthritis,
eyestrain and constipation and, as the salesman grows older,
cardio-vascular disorders.

Another factor frequently referred to as deleterious to health
is the constant change of lodging and eating in a different place
every day.   The fact that travellers frequently have to prepare
their reports, plan future interviews and schedules, etc. in their
hotal rooms outside normal working hours is an additional element
making relaxation difficult.   One union has asserted in particular
that eating in different restaurants (sometimes of indifferent
quality) every day gives rise to a tendency to develop stomach
ulcers.[1]

A third factor is the continual pressure to sell to which all
external salesmen are subject.   Since their performance is judged
by the volume of orders they obtain, there is a continual pressure
on them to make an extra effort, which can be compounded where
management employs the technique of "the traditional sales meeting
and contest, which exhort the salesmen to make one extra call
every day and to dedicate their entire waking hours to the selling
profession".[2]   These pressures can become even greater in times
of recession, when business is low and orders are hard to come by.
They are particularly great where commission represents a substantial proportion of the traveller's earnings.

Lastly, the effects of disruption of a normal family life
deserve mention.   As was seen earlier, the over-all situation
in this regard has improved considerably; even so, continual
and sometimes lengthy absences from home are liable to create strains,
not only for the traveller, but for his family as well.   Similarly,
the need to work at home during weekends is frequently stated by
travellers to have a disruptive effect on their family lives.

As one salesman has put it, "For this kind of work you need
an iron constitution and absolutely unshakeable determination
and morale".[3]

---

[1] Le Mercure (Berne), 15 Nov. 1977.

[2] Stroh, op. cit., p. 173.

[3] Promouvoir, loc. cit., p. 26.

CHAPTER V

REMUNERATION

Introductory

A number of factors combine to make the subject of remuneration of commercial travellers and representatives a particularly complex one.

Firstly, it must be borne in mind that actual remuneration depends to a great extent on individual negotiation between the traveller and his employer. It is true that in a number of countries minimum levels of remuneration are set in legislation or collective agreements, either for workers in general or specifically for travellers; but these minimum earnings levels are usually well below the levels of earnings which salesmen hope to attain; moreover, there are countries in which no minimum earnings level is set, either by law or by collective agreement. In the majority of cases, even where statutory or contractual provisions apply, a traveller's relationship with his employer will be based on an individually negotiated contract; in this respect his position is akin to that of a professional worker - or of an independent commercial agent. Model employment contracts for travellers and representatives are frequently drawn up by employers' associations and by trade unions for the use of their members; but these models understandably give no guidance regarding the setting of remuneration, which is normally fixed by reference to such factors as local custom, the nature of the goods sold, the requirements of the job and the respective bargaining power of the parties.

Secondly, in the great majority of cases there is an element of direct financial incentive built into the methods used to remunerate travellers and representatives, which links the level of their earnings, to a greater or lesser degree, to the amount of business they obtain. This incentive element usually takes the form of commissions on all orders taken (or, less frequently, that of periodical bonus payments for achieving preset sales objectives). This emphasis on incentive is probably due to a considerable extent to tradition, but it may also be a reflection of such factors as the relatively unsupervised nature of much external sales work and a widespread belief that external salesmen not only need them to exert their best efforts but actually want such incentives.[1] The effectiveness of payments of this kind is being to some extent called into question, and in a relatively small, but growing, number of cases remuneration methods are being introduced which sharply decrease direct financial incentive or eliminate it altogether (i.e. in which fixed salary is the principal or sole element); it is nevertheless still true to say that there is an incentive element in the earnings of most travellers and representatives today, and in a number of countries there are even substantial numbers of representatives who, although enjoying employee status in law, are still paid entirely by commission on orders obtained, in the same fashion as a self-employed commercial agent. The inclusion of an incentive element in the remuneration of travellers and representatives is an accepted practice in all countries (and even in certain countries with centrally planned economies, such as Hungary and Poland) where the profession of commercial traveller exists; in one country, Argentina, the payment of at least part of a traveller's earnings in the form of commission is compulsory.

---

[1] D.W. Belcher, op. cit., p. 505.

A third factor, affecting travellers and representatives paid wholly or in part on a commission basis, is the element of entrepreneurial risk which they share with their employers. Although a traveller seeks orders on behalf of and for the account of his employer, and has in theory completed his task (and thus in principle earned his pay) once he has obtained the order, the actual payment of the commission due is frequently subject to a number of factors outside his control, which may lead to a loss of the financial reward for his efforts through no fault of his own. In this regard his situation, notwithstanding his employee status, is akin to that of the self-employed commercial agent, particularly if he is paid by commission alone.

The legislation applicable to the remuneration of commercial travellers and representatives, where it exists, is usually extremely flexible. In countries such as Belgium, Chile and Spain the relevant legislation states that their remuneration may take the form of a fixed salary, commissions, or a combination of the two. In other countries the authorisation is tacitly assumed; thus in the Federal Republic of Germany and the Netherlands there are certain provisions of the law applicable where a salesman receives a commission as well as a fixed salary, while in Queensland (Australia) the state wage award for 1977 contains special provisions for "a traveller who is remunerated wholly or partly by commission". In other countries again, such as France, the law is silent on the matter.

In a few countries, however, there are restrictive clauses. In New South Wales (Australia), for instance, section 6 of the 1977 state award for commercial travellers provides that, with effect from 1 February 1978, no commercial traveller may be remunerated solely by incentive payments. The Panama Labour Code implicitly contains a similar prohibition. In Switzerland, section 349a of the Code of Obligations states that an agreement under which the remuneration of a sales representative consists solely of commissions is not valid unless the commissions constitute a reasonable remuneration for the services of the representative. The restrictive clause in force in Argentina is of a slightly different character; there Act No. 14546 provides that representatives shall be remunerated partly or wholly by commissions on the value of sales effected (thus an external salesman on straight salary is not deemed to be a traveller or representative).

Collective agreements, where they cover commercial travellers and representatives, are also extremely flexible. Such agreements as do cover them do little more, in the field of remuneration, than guarantee them a minimum level of income which is usually considerably less than a good traveller can expect to earn. As regards the composition of the remuneration, agreements tend to be silent or to state, as does the national interoccupational agreement for travellers and representatives concluded in France on 3 October 1975: "The determination of remuneration shall be a matter for free agreement between commercial representatives and their employers".

It can thus be seen that the parties have considerable freedom
in negotiating the remuneration element of a commercial traveller's
contract, and in particular the level and relative importance of
fixed salary and commission.

This chapter describes the different elements which go to
make up the remuneration of commercial travellers and sales
representatives, and their respective importance in total
remuneration.   It then goes on to consider in more detail methods
of payment containing a commission element, the problems to which
the use of these methods give rise and alternative systems of payment in use.   Finally, it discusses the actual earnings of travellers and representatives and their place in national earnings
hierarchies.

Composition of remuneration

The remuneration of salesmen may be - and often is - made up
of a number of elements.

The most characteristic element is that of commission,
defined in the 1977 commercial travellers' award for Queensland
(Australia), as "any financial payment, financial bonus or financial award directly related to the soliciting of orders or business
by an individual commercial traveller", but not including "any
incentive payment, bonus or award periodically made by the employer
on the basis of profitability or performance of the employee ...".

Commission is generally payable on every sale made by a
traveller or representative and on a pro rata basis related to the
amount of the sale.   To the extent that he is paid by commission,
the traveller is thus in a similar position to the piece-worker
and to the commercial agent, both of whom are paid in accordance
with output and output alone.   In particular, this feature permits
a distinction to be drawn between commissions and bonuses, which,
although of an incentive character, are usually payable only for
a specific achievement (e.g. for successful promotion of a new
product or when a preset target has been reached or exceeded) and
are not necessarily of a fully pro rata character.   Thus, a
"commission" payable only on orders in excess of a given value or
volume (which salesmen's contracts occasionally provide for) is more
in the nature of a bonus than of a commission in the true sense of
the term.

In the early days of the profession, when travellers and
representatives usually had the status of self-employed persons,
payment by commission only, with the traveller paying his own
expenses, was the general practice.   Since the beginning of the
twentieth century, however, travellers and representatives have been
granted employee status in increasing numbers and as such gained
access to many of the benefits enjoyed by other categories of
employees.   An element of fixed salary in remuneration is one of
the principal benefits many of them have achieved.   In some
countries the granting of employee status to travellers and
representatives has brought them within the ambit of minimum wage
legislation; in others, as a result of collective bargaining or
new developments in management policies, the numbers of commercial
travellers with a fixed salary element in their remuneration have
steadily risen.

Although official statistics on the subject are rare, and reliable estimates exist for only a few countries, the evidence available suggests that, throughout the world, the most widely used form of remuneration of commercial travellers with employee status consists of some combination of fixed salary and commission.

Where remuneration is made up in this way, the respective proportions of salary and commission in total remuneration vary according to national practice. Thus in Austria and Sweden, it is estimated that the proportion of fixed salary in total remuneration is usually low. This appears to be the situation in a number of other countries. In Hungary, it is estimated at approximately one-third of total remuneration. In Tunisia, where the practice appears to be to restrict fixed salary payments to the amount of the statutory minimum wage, it is reckoned to be of the order of 10 per cent of average earnings in the profession. In contrast, in the United Kingdom the general tendency is to pay a relatively high proportion of earnings in the form of fixed salary; in 1977, according to a sample survey, commission represented less than 10 per cent of total pay in 15.4 per cent of the firms in the sample paying salary and commission, 10-20 per cent in 29.9 per cent and 20-30 per cent in 21.9 per cent.[1] In New Zealand, it is estimated that commissions and similar payments average only 10 per cent of salesmen's earnings. In the United States, according to a survey published in 1978,[2] the most frequently encountered ratios of fixed salary to commission were 80:20, 70:30 and 60:40 in that order.

Practice in this regard may also vary from sector to sector of the economy; in the United States in 1967, the sample survey referred to earlier[3] indicated that the average level of commission and bonus payments ranged from over half of total remuneration in the furniture industry to less than 10 per cent in such sectors as scientific and research instruments, industrial chemicals, electrical equipment (other than motors and generators) and tobacco. Practices also vary from company to company, according to current remuneration policies; and may even vary from one group of salesmen to another according to the product being sold.

An additional element of remuneration should be mentioned here, which is appearing with increasing frequency in some countries, namely performance bonuses awarded to individuals or groups of salesmen. Unlike commissions, which are paid to good and

---

[1] Tack Research Institute: Salesmen's Pay and Expenses, 1977, op. cit., p. 28.

[2] Dartnell Institute of Financial Research: Compensation of Salesmen: Dartnell's 19th Biennial Survey (Chicago, 1978), quoted in John P. Steinbrink: "How to Pay Your Sales Force", in Harvard Business Review, Jul.-Aug. 1978, pp. 111-122.

[3] Richard C. Smyth: "Financial Incentives for Salesmen", in Harvard Business Review, Jan.-Feb. 1968, pp. 109-117.

mediocre salesmen alike on the basis of their actual sales, bonuses
are awarded for specific performance achievements, such as successful selling of a new or "difficult" product, attaining or exceeding
a sales target during a given period, etc.   From the point of
view of management bonus systems offer a flexible means of directing
incentive.   However, since they are awarded in respect of specific
performance items, they are perhaps less of an integral part of
remuneration than fixed salaries or commission.

There is evidence that in some countries bonus payment systems
are to an increasing extent being used to complement, or even to
replace, commission payments.   Certainly in the United Kingdom the
proportion of salesmen on salary and bonus rose from 19.4 per cent
to 27.5 per cent between 1960 and 1977, while during the same period
the proportion on salary and commission only declined from 42 per
cent to 32.3 per cent, having fallen as low as 30 per cent in
1975.[1]

There are in addition increasing numbers of travellers who are
paid by salary only, with or without occasional bonuses.   This
appears to be particularly the case where the payment of commission
gives rise to special problems (such as the capital goods industries)
or where sales promotion is conducted primarily by advertising, and
the role of the salesman is reduced to that of an "order-taker",
as in the cigarette industry in the United States.[2]

According to the sample surveys mentioned earlier, in the
United Kingdom the numbers of salesmen on salary only, after
remaining relatively stable between 16 and 18 per cent of the
total during the period 1960-68, had risen to 25 per cent or thereabouts over the period 1975-77 while in the United States the
proportion, after falling from about 17 per cent in 1968 to just
under 10 per cent in 1973, rose to nearly 30 per cent in 1977.   In
France, too, the number of travellers on fixed salary only is stated
to be rising.[3]

In some countries there are still considerable numbers of
commercial travellers and representatives paid by commission only,
meeting all their expenses out of their earnings, in the same
manner as a commercial agent.   The proportion, however, varies
from country to country.   According to a sample survey undertaken
in the United States, over 20 per cent of companies pay their
external sales force by commission only.[4]   In France in 1978,
it is estimated that over 20 per cent of the travellers and
representatives covered by the special provisions on the profession

---

[1] Tack Research Ltd.:   Salesmen's Pay and Expenses, 1969 and
1977.

[2] Richard C. Smyth: "Financial Incentives for Salesmen",
loc. cit.,   p. 115.

[3] La Tribune libre (Paris), No. 270, June 1978, p.6.

[4] Steinbrink, loc. cit., p. 112.

in the Labour Code - and in particular those selling for more than
one employer - were remunerated by commission only,[1] whereas in
the United Kingdom the proportion of travelling salesmen paid by
commission fell from only 5.5 per cent in 1960 to 0.8 per cent in
1977.[2]   In Belgium and the Federal Republic of Germany, too, the
numbers of employee travellers on commission only are reported to
be very small, while in Sweden it is reported that only one major
firm remunerates its salesmen by commission only.   However, in
considering such figures as are available on this subject it should
be borne in mind that in some countries - such as Spain and Italy -
travellers and representatives with employee status are in a minority in external selling as a whole and that the greater part of
such selling is still done by persons with the status of self-
employed commercial agents.

Commission

Basis for calculation of commission

Where commission is an element of remuneration, one factor
which has to be specified - in the contract of employment or by
other means - is the method by which the commission due on orders
obtained or sales made is to be calculated.

A number of possibilities exist in this regard.   Commission
may be calculated as a percentage of the selling price or of turnover; this is in fact the method most frequently used.   Alternatively, it may take the form of a fixed sum per item, or per unit
of volume or weight, of goods sold.

While a number of countries allow the use of any or all of
these methods of calculating commission, some countries have laid
down rules restricting the choice of method or the details of the
calculation.   Thus in Argentina, the most recent Act concerning
commercial travellers (No. 14546) stipulates that "remuneration
shall consist wholly or partly of commission on the value of sales
made".   The reason given during the parliamentary debate on the
draft text[3] for the inclusion of the word "value" was that this
method of calculation provided the traveller with some protection
against inflation, whereas the use of any other method was liable

---

[1] It has been estimated that there are in France at least as
many travelling salesmen who do not qualify for coverage by the
special legislation as there are who do.   See Le Point (Paris),
20 Nov. 1978, pp. 82-83.

[2] Tack Research Institute: Salesmen's Pay and Expenses, 1977,
op. cit., p.8.

[3] See Anales de legislación argentina, 1958, Vol. XVIII-A,
pp. 183-199.   It is interesting to note that the principal drafter
of the Act, Haroldo Juan Tonelli, had himself been a commercial
traveller for a number of years before entering Parliament.

to leave his commission per unit of goods sold unchanged in money terms while prices were rising. In Belgium the Act of 3 July 1978 states that unless otherwise agreed the basis for the calculation of commission shall be the order of catalogue price or the actual selling price.

In several countries there is an additional stipulation regarding the price to be used as a basis for calculation.   In Uruguay, for instance, the basis is the order price, not taking into account any discounts granted by the employer other than those indicated on the order forms used by the traveller (i.e. discounts of which the traveller and customer are both aware at the time the sale is closed); this provision serves to protect the traveller against loss of commission on account of any special discounts which the employer may grant to the customer after the order has been accepted.   In the Federal Republic of Germany the Commercial Code states (section 87b) that the commission is to be based on the amount actually due to the employer by the customer, exclusive of any discount for cash payment, and that packing, freight and other accessory costs are to be included in the total unless invoiced separately.   However, it appears that discounts conceded in return for regular orders may be deducted from the sum on which the commission due is calculated, since the traveller derives a financial advantage from the arrangement in the form of commission on a greater assured volume of business.   Where value added tax or other sales taxes are included in the price, the commission may be calculated either on the price including the tax or on the price net of tax according to the terms of the individual contract.

The level of commission, where calculated as a percentage of the value of the goods sold, is a matter for agreement between the parties and is generally stipulated in the contract.   It may vary from sector to sector and from product to product, in accordance with such factors as customary practice in the economic sector or the region concerned; the amount of fixed salary the traveller receives; and the product itself (for instance, a higher commission than usual may be paid on a new product being brought to the market for the first time).   In Argentina, Act No. 14546 contains a provision to the effect that a newly appointed traveller or representative shall be paid commission at the same rate as his predecessor; according to the sponsors of the Act, this provision was included to discourage an employer from transferring a traveller who had built up a clientele in an area and was enjoying high commission earnings and replacing him by a new traveller paid commission at a lower rate.

Where set by contract, the rates of commission payable on the goods and services sold are usually unchangeable unless the parties agree to change them - although in New South Wales (Australia) the 1978 wage award appears to allow an employer to reduce commission rates unilaterally provided that he gives the traveller three months' notice of his intention to do so.

Types of business on which commission is payable

Where a traveller or representative is entitled to a commission on orders obtained, it is invariably payable on all orders result-ing directly from his personal endeavours (i.e. the orders he obtains during visits to customers).

In a number of countries, however, he is entitled, in certain circumstances, to commission on orders which, although not actually obtained during a call made by him, are deemed to be the result of his selling efforts. Orders of this kind might, according to the circumstances, include orders obtained directly by the employer or by another employee of the firm or orders sent in directly to the firm by the customer. Commissions paid on such orders are sometimes known as "indirect commissions".

In these countries criteria for the award of commission to travellers and representatives in these circumstances are found in national legislation or collective agreements. Thus in the Federal Republic of Germany, a traveller or representative is entitled by law to commission on all transactions concluded with customers introduced by him for business of a similar kind (this is in fact the same rule as for commercial agents). A similar provision is in force in Austria, but it is applicable only in cases of doubt. In Italy, a traveller is entitled, under the relevant collective agreements, to commission on orders received directly from customers he visits regularly, and in Chile to commission on orders from customers he has visited previously. In Switzerland, however, the law states that entitlement to indirect commission arises only where the traveller has been assigned a particular area or clientele to canvass.

Where the traveller or representative has been assigned an area or clientele for which he represents the employing firm, the conditions for the award of indirect commission are more liberal.

The assignment of an area or clientele generally gives the traveller or representative exclusive rights to canvass that area or clientele for the firm. This exclusivity does not normally prejudice the right of the employer to conclude transactions directly with customers in the area or on the list of customers (as when, for instance, an order is sent directly to him); in the Swiss Code of Obligations the employer's rights in this regard are specifically reserved. However, the traveller is entitled to commission on any order so received and accepted, whether he has previously visited the customer or not. Provisions to this effect are to be found in South Australia (subject to any arrangement under which a local agent may be entitled to a share of the commission), Austria, Belgium, the Netherlands and Switzerland, among others; and arrangements of this kind are standard practice in many other countries, even where the law or collective agreements are silent on the subject. In some countries, such as France and Tunisia, the assignment of an area or clientele is obligatory if the representation contract is to be recognised as a contract of employment. In Uruguay, however, indirect commission on orders received from a traveller's area is payable to him only if he has visited the customer during the last 180 days, or 60 days in the case of a local agent. In some countries it appears that the rate of indirect commission is lower than that for direct commission. In Argentina and Uruguay, however, the law provides that the two rates must be the same.

Acquisition of entitlement
to commission

Practice varies considerably with regard to the definition
of the point in the course of the transaction at which the
traveller or representative is deemed to have earned his commission
on an order or sale.

In several countries (Austria, Ecuador, Ethiopia, Malaysia)
entitlement to commission is gained as and when the customer pays
for the goods sold.   This is the same rule as that traditionally
adopted between commercial agents and their principals, the
former, as an independent agent, thus sharing to some extent the
entrepreneurial risk of his principal.

In a number of other countries, however, entitlement arises
(or can arise, if the parties so agree) at an earlier stage in
the transaction.   In South Australia commission is deemed to have
been earned on the date of dispatch of goods to the customer, and
in the Federal Republic of Germany and Peru, as and when the
employer completes his part of the transaction (i.e. dispatch and
invoicing).   In several countries entitlement arises even
earlier; in Switzerland it arises when the transaction has been
validly concluded; in Belgium, Brazil, Chile, France, the Netherlands and Victoria (Australia) it arises on acceptance or
confirmation of the order (or failure to refuse it within a
stipulated period) by the employer.   In some of these countries,
however, the relevant legislative provisions contain an "unless
agreed otherwise" clause and are thus not mandatory.

However, in some of these countries the entitlement to
commission does not necessarily carry with it the right of the
traveller or representative actually to receive it.   Thus, for
instance, the Swiss Code of Obligations provides that the right
to commission lapses if the customer fails to perform his
obligations under the contract (e.g. does not pay for the goods
ordered or rejects them without good cause) or if the employer
fails to complete performance through no fault of his own (for
instance, if a wholesaler does not himself receive the goods he
has undertaken to deliver).   Similar provisions are found in
legislation or collective agreements in some other countries
(Denmark, Federal Republic of Germany, Panama); while in France
and the United Kingdom the law allows the conclusion of clauses
to that effect in individual contracts.

A commercial traveller or representative to whom this rule
applies is thus in a position - to the extent that his remuneration is made up of commission - where his actual earnings depend,
not only on his skill in doing his job (which is to win orders),
but also on the performance of the contract by his employer and by
the customer - two sets of circumstances which are largely outside
his control.

There are of course cases in which non-performance of a
contract can be attributed to the traveller himself (e.g. in-
accurate transmission of an order, a promise of unrealistic
delivery dates to a customer, placing an order with a customer
about whose solvency he has good grounds for misgiving); but non-
performance will in many cases be due to the action of the employer
or of the customer.

Where non-performance is attributable to the employer, the traveller enjoys a measure of protection in several countries with regard to his commission entitlements. Thus in Italy, under the national collective agreements for commercial travellers and representatives, the entitlement stands if the employer refuses an order without good cause or if the non-performance is due to fault on his part. In France, where the law and the national collective agreement are both silent on the subject, the present state of case law appears to be that, where the contract of service of a representative stipulates that entitlement to commission depends on performance of the contract of sale, commission is not payable if the employer fails to perform, unless he has been negligent or otherwise at fault.[1] The onus of proof rests with the traveller. The situation is similar in the Netherlands. In Brazil the right to commission stands where non-performance is due to deliberate action by the employer after acceptance of the order. In the Federal Republic of Germany the traveller can claim commission in the event of non-performance by the employer save where non-performance is due to circumstances outside the employer's control or where the circumstances of the customer are such as to give the employer reasonable grounds for non-performance. In practice, however, and particularly where alternative employment is not easy to find, a representative may well feel reluctant to press for payment in such circumstances (possibly through court proceedings), since such action could be detrimental to his relations with his employer.

A more specific criterion is used in South Australia, where, under the 1978 revision of the Commercial Travellers' Award of 1974, commission is returnable where the goods sold are returned within one month of dispatch, and in Panama, where clauses providing for the withholding of commission when goods are returned through no fault of the traveller are void.

Where non-performance is attributable to the customer, however, the risk of losing commission, or having to return it, is greater. As was seen earlier, in several countries commission is not payable until the customer has paid for the goods sold; in other countries the inclusion of a clause to that effect in the contracts of travellers and representatives is allowed. In the Federal Republic of Germany, although entitlement to commission arises when the employer dispatches the goods sold, it lapses, or the commission paid is returnable, if the customer fails to perform. In Brazil, the commission is returnable if the customer is insolvent. Practice in the United Kingdom appears to be broadly similar. In Italy, commission reimbursable is in the event of the customer's bankruptcy or insolvency if the amount recovered through the liquidation proceedings is less than 65 per cent of the amount due. In Belgium, however, and in France (in the case of travellers and representatives with contracts providing entitlement to commission on acceptance of the order by the employer), if the customer fails to perform, commission remains payable unless the traveller or representative has been guilty of misconduct or negligence or is at fault in some other way.

---

[1] Cour de cassation, chambre civile, section sociale (Cass. soc.), 12 March 1975: Bulletin des arrêts de la cour de cassation (Bull. civ.), 75-V-140-2; and 76-V-36-1.

Mention should be made here of a practice still found in
some countries, which creates a more formal linkage between the
remuneration of the traveller or representative and the risk of
the entrepreneur - namely the practice known as <u>del credere</u>,
whereby the traveller guarantees the successful conclusion of the
transaction to the employer and undertakes to indemnify him in
the event of non-payment by the customer.   This practice, which
is sometimes found in commercial agency contracts as well, may
have some justification where the traveller is working in a
foreign country and where he has greater knowledge of the local
market than his employer can have;   but with the development of
communications and the consequent ease with which an employer
can seek the advice of credit information agencies throughout the
world, this justification is losing force.   Many unions are
hostile to the practice;   they consider that its subject-matter
falls entirely within the province of entrepreneurial risk and
that its existence opens the way to certain abuses;   it appears,
too, that there is a substantial body of opinion among employers,
at least in member States of the European Communities, that the
practice might be abolished.   In Switzerland, <u>del credere</u> clauses
in contracts of service of travellers and representatives are void,
with the qualification that a traveller who is empowered to take
orders binding on the employer, may, under a written agreement
and against payment of a reasonable additional commission, undertake to reimburse the employer up to a maximum of 25 per cent of
the prejudice suffered by him where the customer does not discharge his obligations.   In some countries the clause is allowed,
subject to restrictions;   thus, in Belgium and the Netherlands
the amount of compensation the employer can claim is restricted
to the amount of the commission due on transactions, or parts of
transactions, written off as bad debts.[1]

The possibility of loss of commission owing to non-performance
places the commercial traveller or representative in a special
position as regards remuneration, since, to the extent that his
remuneration is made up of commission (and especially where he
is paid entirely by commission), he is placed in a position of
risk similar to that of a self-employed commercial agent, notwithstanding his employee status;   for his earnings may depend, not
only on his skill in doing his job (which is to secure orders),
but also on performance of the contract - an element outside his
control.   It is said that some travellers consider the loss of
an occasional commission in this way as an acceptable occupational
risk;   some unions, however, argue that, once the employer has
accepted an order, the traveller's liability should cease.

The legislatures of some countries, as has been seen, have
sought to safeguard the traveller to some extent, maintaining
the entitlement to commission either in the event of the occur-
rence of certain contingencies outside his control or in all
circumstances where he himself is not at fault.   A few countries,
however, have sought to remove entirely the element of uncertainty
from the entitlement to commission of travellers and representatives.
Thus in Chile, Supreme Decree No. 811, dated 1 December 1977,

---

[1] The proposed EEC directive concerning commercial travellers
and representatives contains a clause to the effect that, without
prejudice to his general obligation to exercise diligence and
discernment, a traveller or representative shall not guarantee
the successful outcome of the business he obtains.   This clause
has received widespread support from the employers' as well as the
travellers' organisations concerned.

specifies that commission is due on acceptance of the order by
the employer; provisions in earlier legislation cancelling the
right to commission in certain cases of non-performance have been
omitted from the legislation now in force. This provision has
the effect of transferring to the employer all liability for the
consequences of non-performance as far as the traveller is
concerned. In Mexico, section 288 of the Labour Code provides
that commission may not be withheld if the transaction on which
it is based is subsequently without effect. Similarly, in
Victoria (Australia) Determination No. 5 of the Commercial Travellers Board for 1978 states simply that "all business canvassed for
by a traveller and accepted by the employer as a result of such
canvass from a territory worked by the traveller shall be credited
to the traveller".

As regards the actual payment of commissions entitlement to
which is confirmed, in a number of countries provisions have been
laid down in law or collective agreements fixing deadlines for
payment. Thus in Belgium, unless otherwise agreed, commission
must be paid two weeks after transmission of the monthly statement
of commissions due, and bears interest from the date due; in
Italy at the latest during the month following that in which performance of the contract is completed (in practice it is usually
paid during the month following that in which the invoice is
dispatched); in Brazil not later than three months after acceptance
of the order; in New South Wales (Australia) not later than 21
days after the last day of the calendar month during which the
order was executed. In other countries the rules applicable are
less precise: in Austria and France commissions must be paid at
least quarterly; in Argentina the law simply states that they
must be paid monthly.

If these deadlines are considered in conjunction with the
provisions governing entitlement to commission, it will be seen
that the period elapsing between the date on which the traveller
or representative on commission takes an order and the date on
which he actually receives the commission may vary considerably and
that the linkage in time between the effort made and its reward
can in certain circumstances be extremely tenuous. In Belgium,
for instance, an order is normally considered accepted and commission due on it unless the employer informs the traveller in writing that he refuses the order, or has reservations on it, within
one month of its transmission; the employer gives the traveller
a monthly statement of commissions due to him for the previous
month, and payment takes place two weeks later; the time-lag in
such a system is of the order of two months. However, under a
legal or contractual system in which entitlement arises only after
the customer has paid for the goods - which he may not receive
until several months after giving the order, if the employer has
a full order book or physical delivery problems arise - and payment
is in addition made quarterly, the traveller may have to wait
several months before receiving his commission.

In this respect travellers or representatives paid by commission only are particularly vulnerable. They frequently have to
pay, out of their earnings, not only their family living expenses
but also their own travel, subsistence and other business expenses,
which are incompressible even in times when business is slow.
Persons in this position need a substantial operating capital if
they are to start up or remain in business and in this respect are
on a par with commercial agents, even though they have employee
status in law.

In addition, where delays in payment of commission are substantial, the association of effort and reward in the traveller's
mind may be weakened and an element of personal incentive lost.

In a few countries arrangements exist for the reduction of
this hardship. Thus in the Federal Republic of Germany the
Commercial Code gives the traveller or representative entitlement
to a reasonable advance on commission to be paid not later than
the last day of the month in which the goods are dispatched. In
some others the matter is dealt with by regulations concerning
payment of expenses. In most countries, however, there appear to
be no general regulations on the subject. Mention should also
be made of other factors outside the control of the traveller or
representative which can affect his commission earnings. These
include seasonal influences; price changes imposed by the firm
he represents (or introduced by a competitor); shifts in customer
demand; technological change; changes in company marketing
goals; business-cycle swings; and changes in government
monetary or credit policies.

A representative selling for several employers is exposed to
an additional risk: if one of his employers goes out of business,
or ceases to manufacture the lines of goods he sells, he suffers
a drop in income (which termination benefits where due can only
temporarily offset), but his expenses remain the same, since he
still has to make his regular tours for his other employers. In
exceptional cases the loss of one employer can make the rest of
his business uneconomic and force him to give up working for his
other employers as well.

⚹

⚹   ⚹

Thus the conditions governing the payment of commissions
applicable in a number of countries create uncertainties regarding
their actual payment and the linkage in time between the payment
of the commission and the effort to which it relates. These uncertainties place a commercial traveller or representative with
employee status, who is paid in whole or in part by commission,
in a situation which is less favourable than that of other categories of employees in two respects. First, his entitlement to
reward for his efforts made is subject to a number of factors over
which he has no control. Secondly, the period during which he
has to wait for his reward is variable and - again for reasons
outside his control - may be substantial. These two factors
seem more typical of the relationship between a self-employed
commercial agent and his principal, both accepting an element of
entrepreneurial risk, than of that between an employee and his
employer.

Income guarantees for commercial travellers

There are a number of countries in which arrangements exist
to mitigate to some extent the insecurity of income of commercial
travellers and representatives, or certain categories thereof.

In several countries general minimum wage legislation is
applicable to travellers and representatives with employee status.
This is the case, for instance, in Brazil, Mexico, Panama and
Tunisia.   In some countries, however, certain categories are
excluded: thus in Peru a traveller or representative paid by
commission only is covered by the minimum wage legislation only
if he works exclusively for one employer, while in Chile travellers
on commission only do not appear to be covered by minimum wage
legislation at all.   In Switzerland, where there is no minimum
wage legislation, the Code of Obligations nevertheless provides
that a stipulation in a commercial traveller's contract of service
to the effect that he shall be paid by commission only shall not
be valid unless the commission represents a reasonable remuneration
for the traveller's services.

In some countries the subject is dealt with in collective
agreements.   In France, for instance, where the minimum wage
legislation is not directly applicable to commercial travellers
and representatives covered by the special legislation on the
profession, a traveller or representative working for one employer
is guaranteed a minimum quarterly income, net of expenses, of not
less than 520 times the hourly amount of the minimum interoccupational guaranteed wage.   However, representatives working for more
than one employer are not covered by this provision.   In Italy,
too, representatives working for more than one employer are excluded from the provisions on guaranteed minimum earnings in
the collective agreements for the profession, which only cover
travellers working for one firm.

There are countries in which the minimum remuneration of
travellers and representatives is set at a higher level than the
statutory minimum wage.   This is the case, for instance, in the
Netherlands, where, in 1978, it stood 15-25 per cent higher than
the general minimum guaranteed wage (and a few percentage points
higher than average earnings in manufacturing industry), according
to grade;   and in New South Wales (Australia) where the award for
commercial travellers in force during the early part of 1978 set
the minimum earnings of a country traveller at just under three
times the basic adult male wage for the State, and about 90 per
cent of average earnings in manufacturing industry throughout
Australia.

In Italy, where the minimum guaranteed levels of earnings of
commercial travellers are set under special collective agreements
for the profession, they compare on the whole favourably with the
starting pay of employees classified at similar levels in specific
industries.   In contrast, in Austria, where travellers are
covered by collective agreements for industrial and other economic
sectors, the guaranteed minimum - even for travellers paid by
commission only - is the salary corresponding to the pay classes
in which they are placed;   the guaranteed starting pay in 1977
varied from sector to sector and from wage class to wage class,
but was generally substantially below average earnings in manufacturing industry;   but after 10 to 15 years' service the
guaranteed minimum was in many cases substantially above that
average.

In addition, individual firms frequently operate drawing rights
schemes under which their external salesmen can obtain advances
against commission on future orders, or on orders already obtained
but in respect of which commission is not yet payable.   These

schemes may operate in a variety of ways; for instance, a traveller or representative may be allowed to draw up to a set percentage
of commission on orders already obtained, or he may be allowed a
fixed monthly sum in drawing rights with quarterly or annual
adjustment.   Such schemes, while not giving an absolute guarantee,
nevertheless ensure a regular minimum level of income.

The guarantee of a minimum level of earnings is frequently not
an absolute one.   While under all arrangements of this kind, the
employer makes up any shortfall of actual earnings below the set
minimum, the additional payment, even under statutory provisions,
often takes the form of an advance against future commission
earnings.   Thus in France the national collective agreement for
travellers and representatives states that any payment made by an
employer to make up a shortfall in earnings may be recovered from
earnings in excess of the guaranteed minimum during the next three
quarters;   in the Federal Republic of Germany some collective agreements contain similar provision for recovery of moneys paid to cover
a shortfall of earnings;   while in Denmark recovery is authorised
by law.

In addition, systems based on advances against future commission are potentially dangerous for the traveller or representative
in that, when difficulties arise, they offer stability of earnings
for a limited period only.   If a salesman has difficulties for a
protracted period - in particular owing to any of the factors outside
his control mentioned earlier - he may soon overdraw, and find himself working to pay back debts to the company, with a corresponding
loss of incentive.

If drawing rights arrangements are left out of account, it
appears that, in the great majority of the cases described,
representatives working for several employers are not covered by
the arrangements, legal or contractual, providing some form of
guarantee of a minimum level of earnings.   In this extremely
important respect such persons, although they may enjoy employee
status in law, are thus exposed to risk to a degree similar in many
respects to that borne by a self-employed commercial agent.   In
New South Wales (Australia), however, the problem of income
security for representatives in this situation has been overcome;
under the award in force through 1978, where a commercial traveller
is working for more than one employer (with the consent of all),
each of them is required to pay an equal share of his minimum remuneration;   the award contains no provision regarding recovery.
The problem of insuring a guaranteed minimum level of earnings in
the event of incapacity for work and unemployment is discussed in
Chapter VII.

Verification of the amount of commissions due

In a number of countries the law or collective agreements
require employers to provide their travellers or representatives
with documentary evidence of the amounts of commissions due.
This evidence may consist of statements, copies of invoices sent
to customers, or both.

In some countries express provision exists giving the traveller
or representative certain rights of verification of the amounts due
to him by consultation of the employer's accounts.   Thus in the
Netherlands, the traveller may require the employer to communicate
all information necessary to verify the amount of commission due
and may if necessary seek enforcement of this right in the courts.

In the Federal Republic of Germany and in Switzerland he can require
production of extracts from his employer's accounts on all transactions in respect of which commission is due to him; in the event of
a refusal he is entitled to have the accounts examined, either by
himself or by an expert (in the Federal Republic of Germany at the
choice of the employer), to the extent necessary to verify the
accuracy or completeness of the statement of commissions due.   In
France, the traveller has no right of personal access to the books
but can apply to the courts for verification.

Advantages and disadvantages of commission-based
methods of remuneration; alternative methods

To the extent that a commercial traveller or representative's
remuneration is based on commission on sales, it is directly per-
formance-related and the incentive to sell is high, and from
management's point of view payment is determined by the results
achieved.   This method of remuneration is practised in a very large
number of companies; many travellers actually prefer to be paid
by commission only on account of the high earning potential this
method gives them.   Studies made in the United States indicate
that commission salesmen earn, on the average, about 20 per cent
more in gross pay than those in comparable jobs who are on straight
salary.[1]

However, the adequacy of commission-based remuneration systems
has been increasingly questioned in recent years.   From the standpoint of the salesman, they create the uncertainties already mentioned - to which must be added the insecurity caused by seasonal
peaks and troughs in demand and cyclical booms and recessions in
the market, and also possible inequities arising from differences
in the sales potential of different products and territories.   A
salesman on commission may thus find that the relationship between
his efforts and his earnings is highly variable.   Some of the
objections put up from the management side are that commission
systems create a relationship between the salesman and his employer
which is based primarily on mutual financial interest and which is
not conducive to the development of loyalty; that they may
encourage excessive concentration on selling (leading possibly to
over-selling or skimming the market) and neglect of the non-selling
aspects of the job (such as "missionary" work, technical follow-up
and reporting) which contribute to the building up of the firm's
business; that they create obstacles to mobility of salesmen -
especially good ones who know their territories well; that they
are liable to create situations in which a salesman may be earning
more than his sales manager at head office; that, with their
emphasis on volume, they make it difficult to control the level
of product sales; and that they are unsuited for the growing
number of sectors when the emphasis is on service rather than sales
volume.

---

[1] Sibson, op. cit., p. 148.

In addition, administrative difficulties exist in some branches of the economy. For instance, in the building industry the winning of contracts can be a long and involved business with many decision areas which are geographically dispersed; business generated in one area may show up in the sales figures of another area, and it is not always possible to link the two. In companies manufacturing capital goods, where the number of orders taken during a year are few, and a large number of people may be involved to different degrees in the drafting and completion of any one order, thus making it necessary to determine the share of each individual in the total effort; in such industries, in which the amounts of invoices are enormous and the potential commission earnings and financial insecurity are both high, it is understandable that a commission scheme would be difficult to operate. Lastly, the demarcation of salesmen's territories in such a manner as to ensure a reasonably equal market potential in all may be fraught with difficulties.[1]

A number of companies in different countries have sought to develop remuneration systems for their external salesmen which overcome some or all of these problems. All of them involve the setting of the salary element at a point where it provides a sufficiently significant proportion of total earnings to give an adequate sense of financial security and of loyalty to the company.

Some of these companies have resorted to payment of their external sales forces on a straight salary basis, with no incentive payments based on sales volume or other factors at all. From the standpoint of management, such payment schemes overcome some of the disadvantages of schemes in which commission payments predominate; in particular, they give management greater control over the external sales force, since they allow greater emphasis to be laid on the non-selling aspects of a marketing programme and eliminate certain problems regarding transfers of external salesmen. From the point of view of the salesmen themselves, they provide stability of income and a feeling of financial security. However, they do not contain the direct incentive element which not only many employers, but many salesmen as well, consider to be an essential element of remuneration for the external sales force;[2] it has been argued that the system discourages maximum individual effort, and actually gives salesmen who are earning their maximum salary levels an incentive to start looking for better-paid jobs.[3]

------

[1] On this subject see British Institute of Management: Remunerating Sales and Marketing Staff, Management Survey Report No. 33 (BIM 1976).

[2] One study on salesmen's remuneration made in the United States some years ago revealed that, while employers were showing some increasing tendency to favour salary-based plans, 65 per cent of the salesmen themselves preferred incentive programmes. See Incentives for salesmen: a symposium. Experiences in Marketing Management, No. 14 (New York, National Industrial Conference Board, 1967), p. 14.

[3] Paul H. Nystrom (ed.): Marketing Handbook (New York, Ronald Press, 1958), p. 775.

Remuneration schemes comprising both salary and commission combine, to a greater or lesser degree according to the nature of the scheme, the advantages and disadvantages of both types. However, many companies have found that, even with the most judiciously selected combinations of salary and commission payments, they have been unable to harness the activities of their external sales forces to the furtherance of their marketing objectives - and in particular long-term objectives relating to the building up of a satisfied and faithful clientele - with the degree of precision they would wish to achieve.

In response to this problem a further refinement has been introduced into salesmen's remuneration systems in many firms, involving the replacement or supplementing of commissions by bonuses, payable over and above a base salary set at a level designed to provide salesmen with a reasonable if modest standard of living, and designed to reward the meritorious performance of specific tasks considered of priority importance by the firm concerned. These tasks may be of many kinds. The simplest form of bonus is that paid for achieving or exceeding a preset sales quota; but bonuses may also be paid in respect of such aspects of performance as sales of particularly profitable lines of goods, new lines, or lines which are not selling well; sales during slack periods; sales of a balanced range of goods matching production schedules; the opening of new accounts or the development of existing ones; sales in a difficult or new territory; the performance of specific non-selling tasks such as securing displays, "missionary" work and after-sales service activities; and matching of forecasts with actual sales. In a few cases penalties have also been included in individual schemes - for such occurrences as the loss of a customer (say, six months without an order), bad debts, complaints from customers and returns of goods. Some firms have introduced group bonus schemes, designed, for instance, to even out differences in the degree of difficulty in attaining sales objectives in different territories or to promote team work.

The common feature of all bonus schemes is that they help management, by means of incentives, to direct the efforts of the field sales force more towards the fulfilment of the immediate or long-term marketing objectives of the firm concerned, and also permit the payment of an immediate reward for performance of activities which do not yield an immediate return in the form of new orders, but which may be considered to be essential as investments to consolidate and develop the firm's position in the market. The retention of the incentive element gives them an advantage in this regard over straight salary schemes.

Thus the use of payment schemes comprising both salary and bonus elements offers an extremely flexible method of combining the strengthening of salesmen's feeling of financial security, the maintenance of the incentive factor, and the direction of their effort towards the firm's objectives.

Bonus schemes are frequently complex, and considerable effort is sometimes needed to ensure that they are understood and accepted by the sales force. One factor which has been described as making a major contribution to acceptance is the association of the sales force with the actual development of the schemes.

Although, as seen earlier, increasing numbers of companies
are strengthening the salary elements in the remuneration of
their field sales force and introducing bonus schemes in place of
or to supplement commission payments, the trend is far from
universal. Many firms still consider that financial incentives
in the form of commission are an indispensable tool for managing
and motivating their sales forces, or consider that alternative
systems are excessively complex and not understood by their sales
forces. In fact, when both management and the external sales force
believe that commission-based systems of remuneration work, the
result may be a self-fulfilling prophecy. In addition, a significant proportion of companies which experiment with payment systems
without a commission element eventually return to salary-plus-
commission or commission-only systems. It has even been suggested
that there is a cyclical pattern of change in remuneration
policies.[1] On the workers' side, fears are sometimes expressed
that the introduction of schemes of this kind may create a
situation in which high performance will result in cuts in
incentive rates.[2]

In addition, some unions have expressed misgivings regarding
certain forms of bonus systems, especially those with a strong
competitive element. Thus, the United Commercial Travellers'
Association of Great Britain is opposed to the concept of performance awards for salesmen when organised on a competitive basis
and where only a proportion of a sales force is intended to receive
the awards.

However, the growing number of firms which are going over to
salary-only payment systems suggests the emergence of a new
attitude on the part of many firms towards their relationships
with their external salesmen. In addition to a desire to achieve
greater flexibility in the use of external sales forces there is
evidence, first, of a questioning of the long-term effectiveness
of commission-based payment schemes, and secondly, of attempts to
replace the financial incentive to perform, in part or entirely,
by other incentives, such as strong and helpful management,
opportunities for achieving greater job satisfaction, and closer
involvement in the work of the company (for instance, in such matters as planning of marketing and selling strategies, pricing and
even the design of remuneration systems).

Approaches of this kind have considerable potential as a means
of reducing the feeling of isolation which has traditionally been
the lot of the commercial traveller and of enhancing his status and
the personal satisfaction he derives from his work.

What commercial travellers and
representatives earn

Notwithstanding the importance of pay questions in the context
of the general management problem of attracting and keeping good
salesmen, reliable figures on the earnings of commercial travellers

---

[1] British Institute of Management, op. cit., p. 8.

[2] Belcher, op. cit., p. 515.

and representatives are not easy to come by.   Collective agreements,
where they refer to the remuneration of travellers, only fix a
floor wage, which the individual traveller with a reasonable degree
of selling ability may expect to exceed considerably.   Even in
individual contracts, earnings cannot be determined precisely except
in cases where the remuneration comprises no incentive elements
at all.

In a few countries surveys of salesmen's earnings, based on
information supplied by representative samples of firms, are carried
out regularly, among other things, to provide managements with a
sound factual basis for decisions concerning the pay levels of the
travellers in their employ.   In other countries it is necessary
to go to population censuses (but these do not always distinguish
travellers and representatives as a separate category) or to make use
of estimates.   Frequently, only averages can be obtained, which,
in view of the wide range of earnings within the profession, do
not give indications as precise as one could wish for.   However,
it is possible, from such figures as are available, to arrive at
some tentative conclusions regarding the position of travellers
and representatives in national earnings hierarchies.

Since travellers and representatives are found at a number of
different levels in the occupational hierarchy - from the "order-
taker" to the highly qualified consultant - and since methods of
remuneration vary so much, the range of earnings in the profession
of commercial traveller or representative is inevitably wide.
At one extreme, there are travellers who earn more in a given year
than their supervisors, or even possibly than the managing director
of the firm employing them;   at the other, there appear to be substantial numbers who make a bare living from their work.

In Belgium it is estimated that the highest-paid travellers
earn up to 20 times as much as the lowest paid.   A more specific
estimate can be made of the situation in France by reference to the
statistics of the compulsory supplementary pensions scheme for
commercial travellers covered by the special legislation on the
profession (IRPVRP) and thus travelling full-time;   in 1977, at
the upper end of the range, out of 168,400 contributing members,
2.3 per cent of members declared for contribution purposes net
earnings (i.e. after deduction of expenses where appropriate) of
between 2.5 and 4 times the ceiling of contribution earnings for
the general social security scheme - a ceiling which represented
approximately 1.3 times average earnings in manufacturing industry
during the same year;   while at the other extreme, 42.8 per cent of
the membership declared net incomes of less than half that
ceiling.[1]   In the United States, according to the 1970 population

---

[1] It may be that the numbers of persons in the lowest group
has been artificially swollen by a practice which in some countries
is alleged to be widespread but which is difficult to quantify.
This is the practice said to be followed by some employers of
offering low salaries and commission rates but making up for this
by paying exceptionally large expense allowances.   Within travellers' unions this practice is described as a tax avoidance device
or as a device to reduce employer contributions to the various

(footnote continued on p. 67)

census, the mean earnings of sales representatives in manufacturing were $13,198; but 2 per cent of the total were earning less than $2,000 per year and 9 per cent over $25,000.   Figures indicative of widely ranging earnings levels can be found for other countries.

In addition, it must be borne in mind that in certain sectors an individual salesman's yearly income may be substantially affected by a single transaction.   For instance, the case is quoted in Chile of a representative of a sanitary equipment firm who obtained an order for all the sanitary equipment needed for a large block of flats under construction which brought him commission equivalent in amount to up to a year's normal earnings.[1]

The variable elements present and the extent of the range between the lowest and the highest levels of earnings in the profession make the significance of figures relating to average or median earnings[2] of salesmen and representatives less than that of

---

(footnote continued from p. 66)

social security or pensions schemes to which travellers are affiliated; and there can be no doubt that in certain circumstances it can reduce the earnings basis on which social security and retirement benefits are calculated.   However, in view of the strong individual element frequently present in the negotiation of travellers' contracts of service, the travellers' unions can do little to resist the practice other than through advice to members.   Moreover, such arrangements are not necessarily always and entirely prejudicial to the individual traveller.   As one Swiss commentator has put it: "The contractual rules concerning expenses, commission and fixed salary often give rise to dubious arrangements (setting of expenses at an excessively high level, a small fixed salary, uncertain commissions), not so much to the prejudice of the employee as to help him to keep his costs down by declaring an income which is lower than his real income for tax purposes, where he is required to pay alimony or in the case of distraint on earnings" (E. Schweingruber: Commentaire du contrat de travail selon le Code fédéral des obligations (Berne, Union syndicale Suisse, 1975), p. 279).

[1] El Mercurio, 31 Dec. 1978.

[2] The average is the sum of a set of values divided by the number of values; the median is the value in the set which divides the individual values, arranged in order of magnitude, into two equal parts.   The median figure sometimes gives a more accurate impression of actual magnitudes than the average.

similar figures for other occupations. However, such figures can
show in general terms where travellers and representatives stand
in national earnings hierarchies and to what extent their positions
have changed over the years. This position can be assessed by
reference to a number of factors, such as comparison with average
earnings in manufacturing industry (a frequently used comparison in
pay comparability studies) and with movements in the consumer price
index. The identification of other occupations in which remuneration is similar would be of interest, but in view of the range of
earnings levels within the profession and differences in the composition of pay hierarchies in different countries such a comparison
would have little significance on the international plane.

In the United States, according to the sample survey referred
to earlier,[1] the average earnings of experienced salesmen rose
from $7,200 per year in 1952 to $24,500 in 1977 - 340 per cent above
the 1952 figure. During the same period, average yearly earnings
in manufacturing industry rose from $3,530 to $11,800 - 334 per cent
of the earlier figure. Over the period, the ratio of salesmen's
average earnings to average earnings in manufacturing industry,
which stood at just over 2:1 in 1952, rose to 2.25:1 in 1958,
gradually declined to a low of 1.74 in 1968, climbed back to just
over 2:1 in 1973 and remained stable at that level until 1977.
Over the same period the general consumer price index for the country
rose from 100 in 1952 to 215.9 in 1977. By these two criteria,
travellers and representatives in the United States have in general
maintained their standing in the earnings hierarchy and obtained a
substantial improvement in real earnings. From 1964 until 1976
average earnings were highest among salesmen on commission only;
but in 1977 salesmen on earnings consisting of both fixed salary
and incentive achieved the highest average.

A study of earnings levels as shown in the 1970 population
census[2] throws up other interesting comparisons. The median
earnings of male sales representatives in manufacturing during
the year stood at $11,124, or 132 per cent of median earnings for
all male sales workers ($8,447); only the median for stock and
bond salesmen stood higher. Sales representatives working for
wholesalers earned rather less: the median for this group was
$9,585, or 113 per cent of the median for all sales workers.
A striking fact which emerges from the census figures is the
differentials between the earnings of men and women travellers and
representatives; the median earnings for women travellers and
representatives were only $3,721 in the manufacturing sector and
$3,684 in the wholesale sector. Various hypotheses may be
advanced in explanation of these differentials: for instance, the
group of women travellers may contain a proportion of part-time
workers.

---

[1] John P. Steinbrink: How to pay your sales force, loc. cit.,
p. 117.

[2] 1970 Census of Population: Occupational Characteristics
(US Department of Commerce, Bureau of the Census, 1973).

In France statistics on average earnings are available[1] over
a number of years for representatives working for more than one
employer (multicarte) and covered by the special legislation on
the profession.   During the period 1969-76 the average earnings
of multicarte representatives rose by 112.4 per cent, from 30,153
to 64,060 francs per year;   during the same period average earnings
in manufacturing industry rose by about 140 per cent (from 12,428
to 30,000 francs per year).   Average earnings in the two groups
rose at about the same rate until about 1974, when the earnings of
representatives began to fall behind;   the ratio between the two
averages was of the order of 2.4:1 from 1969 until 1973, but thereafter the differential began to narrow: 2.33:1 in 1974, 2.19:1 in
1975 and 2.13:1 in 1976.   Assuming that average earnings of
multicarte representatives, who are all paid by commission only,
are likely to be slightly higher than those of salesmen on fixed
salary or salary plus commission and/or bonus - as is the case in
certain other countries, such as Denmark and the United States -
it can nevertheless be said that the average earnings of travellers
and representatives in France also stand at approximately twice
the level of average earnings in manufacturing industry.   Since
during the same period the official consumer price index rose by
76 per cent, it may also be said that travellers and representatives
have in the aggregate succeeded in improving their real earnings
appreciably over the period covered.

In Switzerland the Swiss Association of Commerce Employees
has made estimates of the earnings of travellers and representatives
in 1977.   Between the ages of 25 and 29 years, travellers' average
earnings were generally of the order of 39,500 to 45,000 francs
per year;   between ages 30 and 39 the average was 44,500-52,000
francs;   while the average earnings of travellers over 40 years of
age were in the 50,000-61,000 franc range.   Since average earnings
in manufacturing industry during that year were of the order of
24,000 francs per year, it will be seen that the average earnings
of travellers range from approximately 1.5 to 2.5 times average
earnings in manufacturing industry - an observation which corres-
ponds roughly to the position as observed in the United States and
France.

In Sweden, the earnings of technical salesmen in 1976 ranged
from 4,620 crowns per month at age 25 in the lowest quartile to
nearly 10,000 crowns in the highest quartile at age 60.   With
average earnings in manufacturing industry at about 3,600 crowns
per month during 1976 and the probability that salesmen of, say,
repeat consumer goods earn rather less than technical salesmen,
the situation appears broadly similar.[2]

---

[1] Caisse de compensation des cotisations de sécurité sociale
des voyageurs, représentants et placiers (CCVRP); Rapport moral
du Président concernant l'année 1977 (CCVRP, April 1978, mimeographed), appendix 4.

[2] Figures taken from Swedish Employers' Confederation et al.:
1976 Salary Statistics for Salaried Employees, pp. 53-54.

In Denmark in 1977, the net average annual earnings of salesmen ranged from 99,617 crowns in the repeat consumer goods sector
to 119,661 crowns in consumer durables and 118,520 crowns in the
capital goods sector.   The lowest quartile recorded for any sector
was 75,329 crowns (capital goods: salesmen on commission only)
and the highest was 223,141 crowns (consumer durables: salesmen
on commission only).   With average earnings in manufacturing
industry during the same year standing at just under 70,000 crowns,
a picture somewhat similar to that in Sweden emerges.

In the United Kingdom the picture is a different one.   In
this country the general situation of commercial travellers appears
to have declined.   In 1968, according to the sample surveys to
which reference was made earlier,[1] nearly 60 per cent of the firms
covered were paying their best salesmen over twice the level of
earnings in manufacturing industry and 13 per cent and 4 per cent
respectively over three and four times that amount.   By 1977,
notwithstanding pay rises ranging from 35 to 52 per cent during
the period 1975-77, the proportion of firms whose best salesmen
were earning over twice average earnings in manufacturing industry
had fallen to 16 per cent; the proportion of firms whose best
salesmen were earning three and four times the average level of
earnings in manufacturing industry respectively had fallen to 2 per
cent and 0.6 per cent.   A somewhat similar picture emerges when
the average earnings figures are compared with movements in the
cost of living: in none of the five groups of salesmen distinguished in the surveys (salesmen of repeat consumer goods, of durable consumer goods, of repeat industrial goods, of capital goods
and of services) did median earnings in the highest and the
average pay groups fully keep pace with the rise in the cost of
living.   The median earnings of the best salesmen showed the
biggest shortfall; in all the five groups, with the exception of
salesmen of durable consumer goods (who did a little better), it
was of the order of 18 per cent over the 10-year period.

For other countries, statistics of salesmen's earnings have
not been found and in some cases are stated to be non-existent.
However, the impression is widespread that travellers and representatives are, generally speaking, among the best paid of all sales
workers at the non-managerial level.   If the situation in these
other countries is at all similar to that in the countries
described (with the exception of the United Kingdom, where special
circumstances appear to have been present), a reasonably able
traveller or representative seems to have fair prospects of
achieving a reasonably high level of earnings.

---

[1] Tack Research Ltd.: <u>Salesmen's Pay and Expenses</u>, op. cit.

CHAPTER VI

EXPENSES

Types of expenses payable

It is a widely accepted practice, and often a statutory
requirement, that expenses incurred by a worker in the course and
the furtherance of his employer's business are charged to the
employer, who can in his turn deduct them from his income for tax
purposes.

In the early days of the profession, when most travellers
and representatives were treated in law as self-employed persons,
it was usual to expect them to bear their expenses out of their
commission earnings; this is still a widespread practice among
commercial agents, although under some individual contracts the
principal pays the agent a fixed sum as a contribution to office
expenses. However, as travellers and representatives have
acceded to employee status in different countries, payment of
their expenses has increasingly become the responsibility of their
employers. Today in the United States it is estimated that over
90 per cent of companies, and in the United Kingdom 85 per cent,
pay all or some of their salesmen's expenses.

A great variety of items of expenditure incurred by commercial travellers and representatives in the course of their work
are classified, in different countries, as chargeable to the
employer. Travel costs and the cost of board and lodging when
away from home are generally recognised as reimbursable; other
categories of expenditure reimbursable in certain countries and
circumstances include postage and telephone expenses; entertainment; parking costs; items of office equipment (typewriters,
filing cabinets, pocket calculators, etc.); subscriptions to
trade journals; club membership fees; clothing; laundry and
dry cleaning.

The amount of expenditure incurred by a traveller obviously
varies greatly, from little more than local transport expenses for
a local agent working in a single town to more than the total
earnings of a salesman whose travels continually take him from end
to end of an area the size of the United States. General speaking, however, expenses represent a significant proportion of the
total cost of a salesman to his company; a survey of over
16,000 salesmen conducted in the United States in the late 1960s
gave an average level of expenses of about 35 per cent of average
gross earnings.[1] In other countries even higher levels, amount-
ing sometimes to as much as 50 per cent of commissions earned,
are reported.

---

[1] Compensating and motivating salesmen, op. cit., p. 40.

In France the tax authorities allow, for purposes of administrative simplification, a flat-rate deduction of 30 per cent of
earnings, subject to a maximum deduction of 40,000 francs per year
(originally set in 1970 at 50,000 francs, but reduced to the present
level in 1978); but the biggest travellers' union claims that
actual expenses are much higher - of the order of 60,000 francs per
year in an average territory (La Tribune libre, No. 273, Nov. 1978,
p. 10). When these figures are compared with earnings after
expenses (see p. 69) it can be seen that expenses totalling 50 per
cent of earnings are well within the bounds of possibility. It is
also interesting to note that, in the Federal Republic of Germany,
the expenses of commercial agents in 1975 averaged 50-60 per cent
of gross commission earnings, according to the sector (Forschungs-
verband für den Handelsvertreter- und Handelsmaklerberuf: Kosten,
Erträge, Rentabilität der Handelsvertreterfirmen: Ergebnisse der
CDN-Statistik 1976 (Cologne, 1977, p. 4); but the average might be
expected to be rather higher for commercial agents than for
employee travellers, since most agents have one or more employees
(ibid., p. 18); whereas an employee traveller may not employ other
persons.

A variety of means of covering expenditure of this kind exist.
The two principal methods in use are the payment of fixed allowances, either per day or per item of expenditure (meal, night in
hotel) and the reimbursement of actual expenses. In the latter
case, the relevant awards, agreements or contracts usually specify
that reimbursable expenses must be "reasonable" or "justified".[1]
In some cases, where the amount of expenses during a tour can be
approximately estimated in advance, a traveller may be given an
imprest account or a "float" against which he can draw, thus reliev-
ing him from the disagreeable situation of being continually out of
pocket.

One field in which considerable developments have taken place
since the end of the Second World War is that of travel, where the
development of the use of motor cars has brought about radical
changes. While train and air travel are still frequent, the
convenience and reliability of the motor car as a means of travel
from customer to customer and of transporting samples (which may
be bulky) is such as to have made it an almost indispensable tool
of the traveller's trade - with certain exceptions, such as local
agents for certain types of services operating in the centre of a
large town, where a car can be more of a hindrance than a help.
In some countries the salesman without a car is now an exception;
in the United Kingdom, for instance, according to the 1977 sample
survey mentioned earlier,[2] 97.6 per cent of the companies covered
reported that every one of their salesmen used a car.

---

[1] In some awards in Australia a floor level of expenses is
set for some items (first-class hotel accommodation and rail
travel).

[2] Tack, 1977, p. 36.

A variety of methods have been adopted of applying to the use of cars the principle that all expenses arising out of the performance of work must be borne by the employer.

In a number of countries it is customary for employers to make available to their travellers cars bought, leased or hired by the company, which usually (but not invariably) also pays road taxes and insurance and pays or reimburses the cost of fuel, maintenance and repairs or pays a regular annual or mileage allowance to cover those costs. Not infrequently the employer allows the traveller the use of the company car for private travel, either with or without restriction, and in some cases with some form of reimbursement; in the United States in 1977, according to the sample survey mentioned earlier,[1] nearly 60 per cent of all firms (including nearly 30 per cent of all firms paying their salesmen by commission only) had some arrangement of this kind.

Alternatively, the traveller may, with the agreement of the employer, use his own car for his business travel.[2] Where this is the case, the contribution of the employer to the cost of running the car is usually fixed in the individual contract of employment; sometimes the amount and form of the contribution is set by law or collective agreement as a minimum or on a "unless agreed otherwise" basis. Thus in Switzerland the law requires that a worker be reimbursed not only all day-to-day running and maintenance costs connected with employment but also, where the vehicle is used on a regular basis, payment of road taxes and third-party insurance and a depreciation allowance. The methods of payment most frequently used where the traveller provides his own car are the payment of a fixed mileage allowance; the payment of a fixed weekly or annual allowance; and the payment of a basic allowance plus a fixed payment per mile or the cost of petrol, oil, etc. There are also in some countries - and especially in those countries where there are substantial numbers of representatives, working for more than one employer - cases where no contribution to the salesman's car expenses is made. Occasionally, however, a firm will grant a loan to a salesman to enable him to buy a car.

Frequently, however, the allowances given in respect of the use of the salesman's own car do not correspond to the actual cost to him of using it for his work. For instance, a fixed weekly or yearly expense allowance may be a windfall or a penalty, according to the mileage done. Similarly, the car insurance paid by the employer may not cover all possible damage, but leave part to be borne by the traveller himself. On the other hand, the use of a company car for private purposes - even where treated as taxable - can be a valuable benefit for a salesman. In addition, as mentioned, there are cases where no allowance is made. While it may well be that an occult allowance may be included elsewhere in total remuneration (e.g. in commission rates) this procedure has the disadvantage of confusing remuneration, which is taxable, with expenses, which are not.

---

[1] Steinbrink, loc. cit., p. 121.

[2] In some countries ownership of a car is sometimes a prerequisite for employment as a travelling salesman.

The respective merits of the system of provision of a car by
the employer and the traveller respectively were considered in 1975
by the Western Australian Industrial Commission when issuing its
wage award (No. 35 of 1975) for commercial travellers.[1]   Observing
that some 80 per cent of the persons covered by the award were
supplied, at no cost to them, with vehicles by their employers,
which in most cases they could use for private purposes, the
Commission took the view that a worker supplying his own vehicle
should if possible be in a position not less favourable than that
of a worker with a company vehicle.   Consequently, in addition to
normal running costs (petrol, servicing, tyres, battery, repairs)
and standing costs (depreciation, insurance, garaging or washing,
etc.), the Commission added an interest charge, calculated at
savings bank rate on the initial cost of the vehicle, to the total
of car allowances on the grounds that the traveller was providing
a capital item for the employer and in so doing had to forgo the
use of the money spent providing that item.   The interest charge
was designed to place him in a position where he would in theory,
on giving up the profession of commercial traveller, be able to
sell the vehicle and be in much the same position as a traveller
with a company car.

Another major item of expenditure of travellers and representatives is hotel accommodation, meals and ancillary items of
expenditure such as laundry, dry cleaning, etc.   Here again, a
variety of methods are used - refunds of actual costs, fixed inclusive daily allowances, fixed allowances per meal, etc.   As was the
case with transport expenses, there are significant numbers of firms
which, for one reason or another, make no contribution to expenses
of this kind.

Telephone expenses are a charge frequently accepted by
employers in some countries.   In the United Kingdom, for instance,
only about 5 per cent make no contribution to telephone expenses;
but the most usual practice appears to be to refund all business
calls and to pay all or part of the cost of installation and rental.

Entertainment allowances are a subject which has from time to
time attracted adverse publicity - usually in the context of an
exceptional instance of proven commercial corruption - on account of
the real or imagined opportunities for abuse to which they give rise.

Information on the prevalence and amount of entertainment
expenses allowed to travellers is scant and mainly confined to the
United States and the United Kingdom.   In these two countries,
according to the two sample surveys mentioned earlier in this section, 75-80 per cent of the companies covered reported payment of
entertainment allowances to their salesmen.   In the United States,
many companies state that such expenses must have prior authorisation or were of the "luncheon only" type, and that expense limits
were usually set.   In the United Kingdom, while the general
practice appears to be that of reimbursement on presentation of
vouchers, there is evidence that the amount of expenditure is kept
under scrutiny, since during the period 1975-77 entertainment
expenditure per man reported rose more slowly than the consumer
price index.

---

[1] Western Australian Industrial Gazette, 28 July 1976, pp. 801-
811.

Problems encountered in connection with
payment of expenses

While the arrangements made for the payment of employee travellers' expenses seem in the main to reflect adequately the principle that business expenses are chargeable to the employer, there are certain situations in which they appear inadequate.

Mention has already been made of the fact that a traveller whose expenses are reimbursed is continually out of pocket, possibly for a substantial amount. This problem can be dealt with by the provision of an advance or "float", or of a credit card, by the employer.

A more difficult problem arises from the fact that the expenses of travellers and representatives paid by commission only are frequently included on a de facto basis in the commission paid, and thus treated as a part of earnings. In some countries this practice is applied even more extensively; thus in Italy under the national collective agreement for commercial travellers in industry, 50 per cent of any fixed daily allowance a traveller receives is counted as part of remuneration, while in Argentina the law states that all expense allowances shall be so treated.[1] This situation can give rise to tax problems; while the traveller should in normal circumstances be able to show the actual amounts expended as deductible from taxable income, he nevertheless has to carry the extra burden of proving that the expense money is not income; and since absolute uniformity of interpretation cannot be expected from all tax inspectors, anomalies of treatment and feelings of injustice may arise.

An even more serious problem, of which mention has already been made, arises in the case of travellers and representatives paid by commission only. Where payment, and the timing of payment, of their commissions depends on factors outside their control (and in particular payment by the customer), commission may on occasion be lost. As that commission includes an amount for the traveller's expenses, that amount is also lost; but the expense relating to the unsuccessful transaction has already been incurred, and has to be covered out of the traveller's earnings on other transactions. In this respect a traveller on commission only, notwithstanding his employee status, is exposed to the same risk as a commercial agent, without any recourse against his employer. The situation is some- what different where the breakdown of the transaction is due to failure by the employer; here at least the traveller has a recourse. Even so, he is still for the time being out of pocket for the amount of expenses included in the commission, and may have to put out even more money if he decides to take the case to court.[2]

---

[1] This provision may be designed to discourage certain tax avoidance devices of the kind described in the note on p. 66.

[2] In Chile the traveller in this situation enjoys some legal protection; he is entitled to payment of all his expenses if the employer reduces deliveries to 40 per cent or less of orders accepted. A similar provision is in force in Argentina.

A similar situation can arise where the employer of a travel-ler on straight commission instructs him to undertake a special sales drive in his territory.   To achieve this he may have to travel more, stay away from home more, entertain more (and thus spend more) without any hope of recovering the additional expen-diture unless his efforts are successful.   He is thus in the anomalous position of being forced to carry a personal financial risk, in the same way as an independent commercial agent, by the fact of complying with the instructions of his employer - unless the latter is prepared to contribute to the additional expenditure involved.[1]

This situation may partly explain why, for instance, in France (where payment of commission only after successful completion of the transaction is an accepted practice) the largest commercial travellers' union is seeking such concessions as exemption from parking fees and motorway tolls, petrol at reduced rates of excise duty and partial exemption from value-added tax on the purchase of cars for business purposes.   While the cost of these items can be deducted from taxable income, they nevertheless have to be paid for initially;   and in view of this ever-present risk that expenses will not be fully recovered,   it is understandable that the union should seek means of keeping the initial outlay down to a minimum.

In some countries legislative action has been taken to prevent such situations from arising.   Thus in Switzerland any agreement to the effect that a worker shall himself bear the cost of any or all of his necessary expenditures is void.   Similarly, the commer-cial travellers' award in force in New Zealand provides that all approved expenses must be paid or reimbursed to a traveller over and above any payments made to him in the way of earnings.

It is true that, in the case of travellers and representatives on commission only, the rates of commission set are sometimes designed to allow to some extent for the element of risk described. It is equally true that the apportionment of the expenses of a representative with more than one employer could give rise to administrative complications.   However, in view of the problems described, there seems to be a case for seeking ways and means of giving travellers and representatives on commission only the same security as their colleagues enjoying fixed salaries as regards the reimbursement of expenses incurred in the course of their work - as has been done for instance, in Victoria, where the 1978 commercial travellers' award requires the employer of a commercial traveller who is at the same time in the employ of one or more other employers - "to pay to the traveller a sum of not less than one-third of the weekly amount fixed in this determination as remuneration and expenses ...".   Swiss law deals with the matter even more simply by providing that, in the case of a representative working for several employers, each shall pay an equal share of his expenses unless there is a written agreement among them on apportionment.

---

[1] It is interesting to note in this connection that the draft EEC proposal for a Council Directive to co-ordinate the laws of the member States relating to (self-employed) commercial agents contains a provision (article 20) that an agent shall be entitled to reimburse-ment of expenses incurred in connection with special activities (e.g. the cost of an advertising campaign) undertaken on the instruction or with the consent of the principal.   See "Equality of rights for commercial agents", Bulletin of the European Communities, Supple-ment 1/77, pp. 12 and 22.

CHAPTER VII

SOCIAL PROTECTION

Social security coverage

One of the principal concerns expressed by the Advisory Committee on Salaried Employees at its Third Session in 1935 in connection with commercial travellers and representatives was that the regulations issued to define their legal status "should place them under the legislation for the social protection, insurance and welfare of salaried employees".   A similar concern was expressed by the Trade Section of Commercial Travellers of the International Federation of Commercial, Clerical and Technical Employees (FIET) at its conference in 1953;   it recommended that "employee" commercial travellers should be subject to social security, and that in addition the payment of full remuneration should be continued during reasonable periods of illness.

A survey of the position today reveals that, in a large number of countries, travellers and representatives enjoy the same social security coverages as other groups of workers in the same country. This is the case, for instance, in Argentina, Australia, Austria, Brazil, Denmark, Finland, France, the Federal Republic of Germany, Hungary, Ireland, New Zealand, Norway, Poland, Sweden, Switzerland, Tunisia and the United States.   The entitlement may derive from residence (as is the case under the social security scheme in New Zealand) or, as is the case in the majority of the countries where they are covered, from their employee status.   In countries such as France, proof of membership of the general social security scheme is a prerequisite for registration as a commercial traveller or representative.[1]

There are countries, such as Spain, in which travellers and representatives are not all covered by the general social security scheme;   but in that country legislative action to modify the situation is pending.   In the meantime, membership of the occupational scheme organised by the profession itself is compulsory.

In addition, in many countries and in individual firms commercial travellers and representatives are allowed to join occupational or company schemes providing benefits of a social insurance character, supplementing the benefits provided by the general scheme or providing an element of protection when no general scheme exists. In the United States, for instance, company schemes may cover such items as medical and dental insurance for the worker and his family; salary-based life insurance;   travel accident insurance;   short-term and long-term disability insurance;   and pension insurance. In France, the complementary social security schemes for travellers and representatives, while primarily concerned with the provision

---

[1] In some countries commercial agents may be admitted to the general social security scheme, or parts of it, on a voluntary basis. In Italy, commercial agents must be members of the national retirement pension fund (INPS).

of supplementary retirement, disability and survivors' pensions, can also under certain circumstances guarantee repayment of housing loans incurred by members and grant scholarships, loans and out-right gifts to their children in specially deserving cases.   In Spain, the assistance fund administered by the colleges of commercial agents (which enjoys no regular financial support from outside) provides old-age, invalidity and survivors' pensions;   long illness benefit;   family allowances;   birth, marriage and death grants; and accident insurance.

In Italy, commercial agents also enjoy a measure of protection; there is an official agency known as the National Assistance Agency for Commercial Agents and Representatives (ENASARCO) which operates an old-age, invalidity and survivors' pension scheme.   Membership is compulsory, and contributions are levied from principals as well as the agents.

A certain number of administrative problems arise in connection with the inclusion of commercial travellers and representatives within the membership of social insurance and social security schemes.

The first of these arises from the variable element introduced into earnings where commission is payable.   This element creates problems first of all for the calculation and payment of contributions in earnings-related schemes.   To simplify the procedures involved, Austria uses the annual ceiling contribution earnings in force as a basis for calculation of contributions due each month. The traveller's actual earnings are not taken into consideration until the end of the financial year;   at that stage, if the traveller's actual earnings have fallen short of the ceiling, any excess contributions paid are refunded to him.

The problem of calculating contributions is further complicated in the case of a representative working for more than one employer. In France a special equalisation fund has been established to collect contributions due from employers and transfer them to the competent local social insurance funds.

At a later stage, the presence of the variable element in earnings is liable to complicate the calculation of a traveller's or representative's pension.   In particular, the commission earnings of a traveller may decline during his last years of employment; if the pensions payable by the scheme to which he is affiliated are calculated - as is frequently the case - as a percentage of earnings over the final year or years of his career, the amount of the pension paid to him may thus be less than that which the amount of contributions paid by him would seem to justify.   This problem will, however, be less significant where the pension is based - as it is in a number of countries - either on average earnings over the insured person's lifetime or on his best earnings years, revalued to take wage and price changes into account.

Problems can also arise where the social security schemes, or parts of them, are not applicable to all categories of employees. The complications which may arise in this regard can be illustrated by an example from Italy.   In that country the workmen's compensation scheme covers primarily manual workers, but commercial travellers are, under a decree dated 30 June 1965, included as a special category within the scope of the scheme provided that they regularly use, in the exercise of their functions, a motor vehicle which they drive personally.   However, some uncertainty remained after the entry into force of the decree as to whether this scheme could be compulsorily applied to commercial travellers (who are not manual workers) and to their employers.   The position was finally made clear by a court decision[1] to the effect that the obligation of insurance is based, not on the job title or principal duties of the employee, but on the fact that, in the course of his duties, he is required to drive a motor vehicle;   thus a traveller must be covered by the scheme, even if he only has to drive a car occasionally.   Travellers who do not use a car at all do not appear to be covered.

As regards occupational or company schemes, commercial travellers and representatives have the same problems regarding transferability of accumulated rights as other categories of workers, but possibly to a greater degree to the extent that they tend to be more mobile.   In the United Kingdom, for instance, the United Commercial Travellers' Association of Great Britain has called for legislation to achieve the transferability of pensions as a statutory right.   However, the problem has been overcome, in part at least, by other methods in certain cases;   thus in the Federal Republic of Germany, for instance, under a 1974 Act for the improvement of company retirement schemes, where a worker leaves the service of a firm before reaching retirement age but after completing a stipulated qualifying period of service, his accrued pension rights must be revalued in accordance with changes in the cost of living.

Special problems may arise for travellers and representatives working abroad, or working in one country for an employer with no office in that country.   In the latter case, they may be required to be members of the national social security scheme and have to assume responsibility for payment of employer contributions as well as their own.   In addition, commercial travellers and representatives working abroad have the same problems as other groups of workers with regard to the transfer to their home countries of pension entitlements built up abroad.   Lastly, if they are posted abroad for a considerable period, they may not be able to maintain or accumulate entitlements in their home countries;   this can be of considerable importance in the case of pension entitlements and where the standard of protection in the country of residence is lower than in the home country.

Sick pay

Provision exists in a number of countries for the continued payment of remuneration by the employer - independently of any cash benefits which may be due under general social insurance or social security regulations - during a limited initial period of incapacity for work caused by sickness or accident.   These arrangements may derive either from general legislation, applicable to travellers and representatives by virtue of their accession to employee status, or from collective agreements or awards applicable either to all the employees in a company or to travellers and representatives specifically.

---

[1] Corte di Cassazione, Sezione Lavoro, 22 April 1974, No. 1132.

The period during which sick pay is due tends to increase with
the length of service with the same employer.   In Argentina, for
instance, full pay is maintained for 3 months for an employee with
up to 10 years' service and 6 months for an employee with over
10 years' service;   while under the 1975 interoccupational agreement for travellers and representatives the period rises from
45 days after completion of the initial 2-year qualifying period
to a maximum of 90 days after 20 years.   Under wage awards currently
in force in Australia sick leave entitlements accrue at the rate
of a set number of days per year and may be carried forward.   In
some countries the amount payable decreases as a function of the
length of the period of incapacity.

The method of calculating the amount payable, and in particular
the method of taking the commission component of a traveller's
earnings into account, varies from country to country.   The collective agreements for commercial travellers and representatives in
force in Italy provide that the reference basis shall be "actual
remuneration";   in Argentina the basis used is average earnings
over the last six months;   while in Denmark, in the case of salaried
employees paid by commission, it is defined as the amount which
the employee would have been likely to earn by way of commission
if he had not been incapacitated.

However, the arrangements made for sick pay do not always
fully make up lost earnings.   Thus, for instance, in France the
1975 collective agreement referred to earlier leaves out of account
earnings in excess of the ceiling used for the purposes of the
retirement pension scheme for managerial and supervisory staff.
In addition, although benefit is payable from the sixteenth day of
incapacity onwards, it becomes due only if the incapacity exceeds
two months in duration.   Waiting periods are found in other
countries as well.   There are also cases where sick pay is based
exclusively on the fixed salary element in remuneration;   a
traveller whose fixed salary represents only a small proportion of
his earnings is liable to suffer considerable hardship where this
rule is in force.   Lastly, in Japan days of absence due to sickness
may in some cases be deducted from the annual holiday.

In view of the purpose of these arrangements - the maintenance
of income during periods of temporary incapacity - certain safeguards are sometimes introduced to ensure that a traveller or
representative does not actually derive financial advantage from
the situation.   This seems to be the reasoning behind the guidelines
in force in Switzerland, where an employer is allowed to deduct from
his own payments to the traveller or representative the amount of
payments received by the latter for the same contingency from other
sources;   thus he may deduct the amount of the benefit paid by a
voluntary insurance scheme if he has paid at least half the premiums.
It may also explain why in some countries the right to indirect commission lapses during the period of incapacity (the right to commission on orders obtained personally by the traveller but on which
commission falls due during the period of incapacity remaining
unaffected).

The arrangements in force concerning sick pay are often
accompanied by provisions to the effect that an incapacitated
traveller's job must be kept open for him for a specified period
following the onset of incapacity.   While the situation of
employee travellers and representatives in this regard does not

appear to differ significantly from those of other categories of
workers, it is interesting to observe that the collective agreements
for commercial travellers and representatives in force in Italy
provide that, in firms of a certain size, a traveller or representative whose employment has been terminated on account of an employment
injury permanently incapacitating him for external sales work may,
within the three months following termination, request re-engagement
by his former employer in any suitable type of work which he is able
to perform.   Inasmuch as a considerable number of travellers and
representatives initially join the external sales force by transfer
from the internal services of their respective firms, this procedure
can offer a form of vocational rehabilitation beneficial to both
the traveller and his employer.

CHAPTER VIII

TERMINATION

In many countries the commercial travellers and representatives to whom employee status has been granted now enjoy in law
the same entitlements and safeguards in respect of the termination
of their employment as other workers in the same country. This
is the case, for instance, in Argentina, Australia, Austria,
Belgium, Brazil, Denmark, Ecuador, Hungary, Ireland, Malaysia,
the Netherlands, New Zealand, Panama, Peru, Sweden, Switzerland
and the United Kingdom.

In a few countries (France, Norway, Sweden) employee commercial travellers enjoy more favourable conditions regarding notice
of dismissal than employees in general, either under special
labour legislation (France) or under general legislation on
commissions (Norway) or commercial agents (Sweden).

These entitlements and safeguards may include, according to
the country concerned, the obligation, on the part of the employer,
to follow a set dismissal procedure laid down by law; to allow
an employee a hearing (and if necessary assistance during the
hearing), or to consult the works council or seek the approval of
the labour administration, before giving formal notice of termination; to give due notice of termination; and to pay termination
benefits as appropriate; and the right of the employee whose
contract is terminated by his employer to seek legal redress
through the labour courts if he considers that he has been dismissed unfairly. The safeguards and entitlements relate to both
individual dismissals and to collective terminations of employment
on grounds relating to the economic situation of the employing
firm.

The position of the commercial travellers and representatives
to whom these measures apply has certainly been greatly improved
as a consequence. However, the peculiar nature of the relationship between a traveller or representative and his employer still
leaves a certain number of problem areas which can give rise to
considerable difficulties for individual travellers. The problems
in question relate to the causes of termination; the indemnities
due to a traveller or representative on termination; and possible
restrictions on freedom to take up other employment after termination (the non-competition clause, or the radius clause).

Special problems regarding causes of termination

The factors which may lead an employer to seek to terminate
the contract of employment of one of his travellers or representatives include those which would move any employer to take similar
action in respect of any of his employees. These include a
demonstrated and continuing inability to achieve reasonable standards of performance (measured by the volume of orders brought in,
taking into account market conditions); serious neglect of duty

(for instance, failure to report essential information on the solvency of a customer); persistent disobedience to instructions; disloyal or dishonest behaviour (acceptance of representations of articles which may compete with those sold by the employer without the latter's permission, transmission of bogus orders);[1] and others. He may also seek to dismiss field sales staff in the event of general staff reductions required, for instance, by the closure of part of the enterprise or by a merger with another firm.

Paradoxically, too, problems may also arise between an employer and one of his field salesmen because the latter is doing well at his job.

When discussing the problems of commercial travellers, one frequently hears of cases of individual field salesmen earning more than their sales managers - or even of the managing directors of the firms employing them.[2] The difficulty of persuading a sales-man in such a position to return to headquarters was mentioned earlier. In addition, such a situation can easily give rise to resentment and morale problems among headquarters' staff.

While some managements are prepared to accept situations of this kind on account of the high levels of sales obtained, others seek to prevent them from arising by the use of carefully thought out pay schemes in which the starting point is the amount the firm feels it reasonable to pay, and can afford to pay, an average salesman for the level of performance desired, the objective being to keep the range of earnings of salesmen within acceptable bounds. Where a salesman's earnings are consistently and substantially above the upper limit of the acceptable range thus set, he may be offered an alternative method of remuneration which, while bringing his total earnings within the acceptable range, it is hoped that he will nevertheless accept on account of other bene-fits offered (e.g. high fixed salary, more generous expense allowances, etc.).

The reaction of the traveller concerned to such a proposal will vary according to his individual concerns and priorities. If he is interested in income stability or admission to the permanent staff, he may accept the new terms proposed, even though a cut in take-home pay is involved. If he is of a more indepen-dent or entrepreneurial disposition he may refuse.

In some countries of Western Europe the commercial travellers' unions state that during recent years the problem has sometimes been approached in a different fashion, namely by attempts on the part of employers to induce their field sales employees to change their status from that of employee to that of independent

---

[1] These examples are taken from W. Froelich and H.H. Eberstein: Der Handelsvertreter-Vertrag (Heidelberg, Recht und Wirtschaft, 1966), pp. 59 ff.

[2] See for instance Smyth, loc. cit., pp. 111-112.

commercial agent.   One consequence of such a change is that the
employer is no longer liable for payment of social security contributions and other social charges in respect of his former employee.
Again, however, there may be cases in which the employee will
prefer such an arrangement on account of the greater independence
it will give him.

Where the traveller does not agree to a change, an employer
seeking to cut selling costs may well be tempted to seek by various
means to bring about the termination of the employment relationship.

An employer who for any reason wishes to end his contractual
relationship with one of his salesmen has, of course, the option
of terminating the contract himself;   but dismissal of an employee
who has not given sufficient cause of dissatisfaction to justify
such action is liable to involve him in a claim for compensation
for wrongful dismissal and, in certain countries, for goodwill
indemnities as well.

A less direct manner of achieving the same end is to create
a working environment for the traveller such that he will terminate
the contract of his own volition (a proceeding sometimes referred
to as "constructive dismissal").   An employer seeking to bring
about such a situation has various means of harassment available
to him;[1] but unless these measures taken actually involve a breach
of the law, the relevant collective agreement or the contract of
employment, the traveller may have difficulty in obtaining redress
(by, for instance, application to a court of law to have the contract annulled);   moreover, the recourses open to him usually
involve termination of the contract with compensation rather than
restoration of the status quo ante.   This will be particularly
the case where - as sometimes occurs - a traveller is employed on
the basis of a vague verbal understanding or a written contract or
letter of appointment which is unspecific or silent on such matters
as the exclusive right to visit an area or clientele to be
covered, scheduling of journeys, reporting requirements and expense
allowances.

---

[1] A perusal of a French legal journal (Recueil Dalloz-Sirey)
provides a number of examples of action of this kind;   where, for
instance, an employer allows other travellers to seek orders in
the area assigned exclusively to the traveller concerned
(Informations rapides, 1976, p. 210) or allows another company
owned by him to sell the same goods as his traveller in that area
(ibid., 1973, p. 247);   or requires his traveller to sell at
higher rates than local wholesalers, thus reducing the traveller's
clientele (ibid., 1976, p. 11) or neglects orders obtained by the
traveller or fails to pay him commission on orders obtained (ibid.,
1973, p. 19) or slanders him to his customers, thus making good
relationships impossible (ibid., 1976, p. 148).

Provisions are sometimes found in the law[1] and in collective agreements[2] concerning commercial travellers which offer safeguards against certain types of pressure which can be exerted.   In addition, the unions to which travellers and representatives belong can often intervene effectively in specific cases; however, the scope of their intervention is limited to their members or to firms in which they are recognised.   An individual traveller or representative who is not a union member - and in some countries these form the majority of the profession - has no one to defend him but himself and is particularly vulnerable to pressures of the kinds referred to.

Financial entitlements on termination

Service benefits: outstanding commission entitlements

A commercial traveller or representative with employee status enjoys the same entitlements as other employees - provided that he meets the necessary qualifying conditions, such as the completion of probation or of a minimum period of service - with regard to termination benefits.

These benefits generally consist of various forms of service benefit, the amount of which will vary according to the length of service of the employee and practice in the country concerned. He will also be entitled, where appropriate, to compensation in the event of redundancy or for unfair dismissal under the procedures applicable.   In addition, in countries with unemployment insurance schemes, a traveller or representative with employee status and who meets the necessary conditions will be entitled to benefit.

Since termination benefits are calculated on the basis of remuneration at the time of termination, special arrangements are necessary where part or all of a traveller's remuneration is made up of commission.   The practice most frequently encountered in such cases is the adoption as a reference basis of average monthly commission earnings over a given period - for instance, the last 12 months.   In Italy, however, the reference period is the last three years.   In countries where the rate of inflation is high,

---

[1] For instance, in Austria the Salaried Employees' Act gives a traveller entitlement to compensation where he is prevented, in a manner contrary to the terms of his contract, from earning commission.

[2] For instance, section 67 of the Italian national collective agreement for travellers and representatives in commerce states that, where a traveller whose remuneration comprises an element of commission is kept at the company's offices for more than one-third of the time when, under the terms of his contract, he should be travelling, he may if he so requests be deemed to have been dismissed without due notice and claim all the indemnities due in such a case.

the averaging of commission earnings over a long period without
any adjustment of those falling within the early part of the period
can substantially reduce the real value of the termination benefits
paid - unless some method of revaluing past commissions is used.

In addition to the termination payments described so far,
commercial travellers and representatives, or some categories of
them, are entitled in some countries to special termination payments
deriving from the particular nature of the system by which they are
remunerated and the particular nature of the contribution they make
to the prosperity of the firms for which they work.

It will be recalled that, where a traveller or a representative is paid partly or entirely by commission, the time-lag between
the completion of his work - the obtaining of an order - and the
receipt by him of the commission due in respect of that order may
be considerable.   Particularly in systems in which the entitlement
to commission becomes effective only when the customer pays for the
goods, entitlement may not arise until several months after
termination has become effective.   It is usual for these entitlements to stand, irrespective of the grounds for termination, since
they represent a payment for work actually done.

Apparently to avoid excessive hardship for a traveller who
might otherwise have to wait several months for commissions on
business not completed at the time of termination, Swiss law
provides that commission on all orders concluded or sent in,
regardless of whether or not they have been accepted or filled, is
payable at the time of termination.

Where an order is to be filled in instalments and commission
on that order is also payable in instalments, it appears to be
customary to pay commission on instalments delivered after termination.   A time-limit is sometimes set for payments of this kind;
in Belgium it is six months.

In a few countries - for example, Belgium, France and Sweden -
the law grants commercial travellers and representatives the right
to commission on orders sent in by their former customers for a
certain period following termination where the placing of those
orders may reasonably be deemed to be the outcome of the efforts
of the traveller.   This may occur, for example, where a traveller
with exclusive rights for an area is not immediately replaced
following termination, but orders continue to come in from that
area.   The period varies according to custom in the country and
the branch of industry concerned;   in the countries where such
systems are in operation, three months appears to be the generally
accepted period;   in France in special cases it may be as long as
three years.

Assessment of the extent to which orders received after the
departure of a traveller can be attributed to his activity while
employed is sometimes a difficult task, especially where - as
appears to be the case in Belgium - the onus of proof rests with
the traveller.   In Sweden a compromise solution to the problem
has been devised;   if the calculation of the exact amount of
orders falling under this head proves impossible, a payment of
three times the traveller's average monthly earnings during the
12 months before termination may be awarded.

The above entitlements apply only to travellers and representatives receiving all or part of their remuneration in the form
of commission.   A traveller on straight salary, or on salary and
bonuses, is considered to have been paid for his work as he has
performed it and to have no further claim against his employer in
respect of orders completed, accepted or received after the date
of termination of his contract.   In France, entitlement to commission on orders received after termination extends only to
travellers and representatives to whom the special legislation on
the profession applies.

The goodwill indemnity

In a few countries some categories of commercial travellers
and representatives are entitled, on termination of their employment, to a financial benefit which stands somewhat apart from
termination benefits generally, namely the goodwill indemnity, or
clientele allowance.

Goodwill indemnities, where payable, are a recognition of the
personal contribution made by the traveller or representative to
the prosperity of the firm employing him, and of the financial
prejudice sustained by him on termination.

The origin of the practice of payment of goodwill indemnities
dates back to the time when external selling was carried out mainly
by persons with the legal or de facto status of commercial agents.
The payment appears to have been based on the argument that the
customers in an agent's clientele buying the principal's goods
were the agent's customers rather than the principal's and that,
on ceasing to sell for the principal, the agent made over to him
the clientele he had built up;   in return for this he was entitled
to a financial consideration based on the future value of that
clientele to the principal.   The payment of goodwill indemnities
in such a situation is still a generally accepted practice where
firms conduct their external selling through self-employed commercial agents.

In many countries the attainment of employee status by
commercial travellers and representatives has led to the loss of
entitlement to a goodwill indemnity on termination, apparently
on the grounds that, since they are working for an employer, any
new customers they bring in are the employer's customers.

In a few countries, however, the legislature or the courts
have upheld the right of an employee commercial traveller or
representative to a financial consideration in respect of the new
business which his employer will receive after his departure as a
result of his efforts while in employment on the basis of a
redefinition of the subject-matter of the indemnity.

In France, for instance, the legal position has been stated
in a court decision[1] as follows: "The [goodwill] indemnity is not
the price paid for the transfer of a clientele, transferred as an
asset from the ownership of the representative to that of his

---

[1] See Droit social (Paris), 1965, p. 247.

employer; its sole purpose is ... to provide, for a representative whose contract is terminated as a result of circumstances outside his control, compensation for the prejudice he suffers as a result of his departure from the firm in that that departure causes him to lose from then onwards the benefit of the clientele he has brought in, created or developed."

In Belgium a similar position has been adopted: the goodwill indemnity "is intended to compensate, on a lump-sum basis, the specific prejudice resulting from the loss of the commissions which the representative might have earned from the clientele he has himself brought in".[1]   In Argentina, the position is less clear; the sponsors of the 1957 Act, in introducing the clause concerning the goodwill indemnity, spoke of the injustice arising from the fact that dismissal of the traveller left his employer with "a ready-made clientele with whom he can continue to have dealings" while the dismissed traveller "is deprived of the clientele into which he has put his entire personality but has no redress".[2]

It will be observed that the entitlement applies only to the prejudice caused by termination due to circumstances beyond the representative's control.   Thus in France, a representative is not entitled to a goodwill indemnity if the termination is due to his resignation or to his dismissal on grounds of serious misconduct.[3]   Similarly, the courts in France have ruled that a traveller or representative on retirement is entitled to the indemnity if retirement takes place on the initiative of the employer, but not if it is of his own volition.   In Belgium, where a similar indemnity, known as the indemnité d'éviction, is payable, a traveller is not deemed to suffer any prejudice on retirement and is therefore not entitled to the indemnity if termination is due to voluntary retirement; however, entitlement exists where a traveller is compelled to withdraw permanently from field sales work on account of incapacity caused by sickness or accident.   In addition, the entitlement is not affected by subsequent employment in a sector other than external sales.

In the cases observed where an entitlement to a goodwill indemnity is established by law, the latter relates it to the personal contribution which the traveller or representative has made to the clientele or the volume of business of the firm employing him.

The calculation of the amount thus due requires consideration of a variety of factors, such as the numbers of new customers brought in by the traveller and the value of their business; improvements in the volume of business obtained by him from

---

[1] Brussels Labour Court, 24 November 1976; quoted in Revue de droit social, 1977, No. 2, p. 127.

[2] Anales de legislación argentina, loc. cit., p. 199.

[3] In Argentina, however, the law provides that the indemnity is payable irrespective of the cause of dismissal; while in Tunisia it is payable only where there has been no fault on the part of the traveller.   In Belgium a resigning traveller can claim the indemnity if he can prove serious misconduct by the employer.

customers who were buying from the firm prior to his appointment; the fidelity of the new customers (e.g. new customers who do not place orders) may not be counted regularly; any losses of previous customers occurring during the period of the employment, the reasons for those losses and the extent to which they may be attributed to the actions of the traveller; any special assistance given by the employer to develop custom in the traveller's area and to which part of the expansion of custom might be attributed; any special payments (bonuses, etc.) made to the traveller in respect of increases in custom during the course of his employment; whether any commission paid included an element to cover expenses; and whether or not the reference period proposed for the calculation of the indemnity was one of normal business.

It can thus be seen that the determination of the amount of the goodwill indemnity can be a complex task, and that if the matter has to be referred to a court of law owing to failure of the parties concerned to agree, protracted and costly investigation may be necessary. The legislatures of some countries have therefore simplified the procedure for establishing the amount due. Thus in Argentina and Uruguay it has been set uniformly at 25 per cent of the amount which would have been payable in the event of unfair dismissal, while in Belgium it is set at three months' pay for a period of service of between one and five years' duration and an additional month's pay for every additional period, or part of a period, of five years. In France, where the provisions of the law are supplemented by provisions in the national collective agreement for the travellers and representatives to whom the special legislation applies, the latter allows the traveller the option claiming the indemnity, to be calculated in the conventional manner, or (if the employer agrees) of waiving it and receiving instead a special termination benefit calculated in accordance with a prescribed formula. The factors taken into consideration are final earnings and length of service; a more favourable weighting is given to the earlier years of employment. In the most advantageous of cases this benefit may amount to ten months' earnings. While the amount of the benefit is frequently less than what might be awarded under the conventional procedure, this method offers the advantage that the money is paid immediately and that expert investigation and court procedures, and the ensuing expense and delay, are avoided. Union officials estimate that about half of all travellers and representatives entitled to a goodwill indemnity avail themselves of this method of settlement.

Mention should be made of another aspect of the decision of the French court mentioned earlier in this section, which laid down the principle that a traveller on straight salary receives payment for his contribution to the volume of the employer's business as part of his salary and is therefore not entitled to a goodwill indemnity. In addition, the right to the indemnity applies exclusively to travellers and representatives to whom the special legislation on the profession applies; those covered by general legislation only - estimated as mentioned earlier, at 40-50 per cent of the members of the profession - have no entitlement in this regard.

*

*　　　*

The problem of payment of goodwill indemnity to a traveller whose employer enjoys the benefit of the additional business he has brought in for a considerable period after his departure resembles in some respects that of the entitlement to compensation of the employee inventor, whose inventions may bring to his employer substantial benefits, sometimes exceeding by far the remuneration of the inventor, and over periods possibly running substantially beyond the term of his employment.

The comparison can be pursued only to a limited extent. In particular, a traveller or representative paid partly or entirely on a commission basis will if he remains with his employer, reap the benefit of his efforts in the form of additional commissions: a situation comparable with that of the salaried inventor will only arise when his employment is terminated. Moreover, under the definition accepted in French case law and quoted earlier, the goodwill indemnity is more of the nature of a compensation for loss of future earnings due to circumstances outside the traveller's control than of a reward for a creative contribution to the prosperity of the employer's business. There is a greater similarity between the position of a traveller on salary alone and that of the employee inventor.

Notwithstanding the sharp differences of opinion which exist on the subject, the view that a traveller or representative is entitled, on termination of his employment relationship, to some kind of reward in respect of the added value accruing to the employer as a result of the increase in the latter's clientele which the traveller has brought about by his efforts seems to be gradually gaining wider acceptance. In particular, within the European Economic Community, the draft proposal for a directive concerning equality of treatment for commercial representatives contains a clause which, if finally adopted in its present form, would establish the right of all such persons to receive on termination, and regardless of the cause thereof, goodwill indemnity not less in amount than that of the termination benefit payable to a person of equal seniority under the laws, regulations or collective agreement applicable, this entitlement to be transmissible to the employee's heirs. As at present travellers and representatives with employee status enjoy entitlement to goodwill indemnities in only two of the nine member countries of the EEC (France and Belgium), the adoption of such a provision would mark a substantial advance towards wider acceptance of the principle.

The radius clause

Content of radius clauses

During the employment relationship a commercial traveller or representative, like employees in general, is expected to refrain from all acts prejudicial to his employer or employers or likely to affect their competitiveness. This obligation precludes, among other things, acceptance of representation of goods or services competing, or liable to compete, with those of his present employer or employers. For this reason the contract of employment of a traveller or representative frequently contains a clause requiring the employer's consent for the representative to take on additional lines of goods.

This obligation lapses with the termination of the contract of employment. However, in view of the special relationships which often develop between a traveller or representative and the customers he visits - for whom he frequently "represents" the firm employing him in a very real sense - an employer may feel that, if one of his salesmen leaves him to go to work for (or to set up) a competing firm, he may be followed by some or all of "his" customers. (This preoccupation can be especially acute where the employer is required to pay the traveller a goodwill indemnity on termination.) In such circumstances he may seek means of restraining the traveller from business activities competing with his own after the termination of the employment relationship in order to protect his own business.

To this end, employers frequently include in the contracts of employment of their external sales personnel clauses prohibiting them from undertaking certain activities, after the termination of the contract of employment, which the employer deems to be in competition with his own business, in much the same way as some employers seek to prevent certain highly qualified employees with a special knowledge of the firm's technical secrets from placing that knowledge at the disposal of a competitor.[1]

The factors the employer seeks to protect are somewhat different from those to which highly qualified employees in general have access. Except in special cases involving high-technology goods or services - for example, where the traveller needs a knowledge of his firm's manufacturing processes so as to be aware of the scope for adaptation of the product to the customer's special needs - travellers and representatives do not normally need to have an extensive knowledge of their employer's manufacturing processes. The special knowledge he does have relates to the employer's business and marketing practices and policies and also, and more particularly, to the employer's customers - their special problems, needs and preferences and other information deriving from the relationship of mutual trust which a good traveller will succeed in developing with his customers.

The conditions of the prohibition vary from case to case. Geographically, it may cover only the area in which the traveller is employed, that area and adjacent areas, or the whole country; in time it may cover one, two or more years or the traveller's lifetime; the range of goods or firms covered by the prohibition may be narrow or, alternatively, extremely wide; provision for compensation may or may not be made; and penalty clauses may or may not be included. In extreme cases a traveller may on termination find himself seriously hampered in finding new employment, or even effectively debarred from the exercise of his profession, for a protracted period.

The radius clause usually becomes automatically operative on termination of the contract of employment, irrespective of the cause - mutual agreement; resignation; and termination by the employer with regular notice.

---

[1] A discussion of the problem of the radius clause in its general application will be found in Roland Cuvillier: "Non-competition and non-disclosure obligations: bond or bondage for the employee ?" in International Labour Review, Vol. 115, No. 2, Nov.-Apr. 1977, pp. 193-209.

However, there are certain cases in which termination does not automatically activate the radius clause.   Thus, in Australia and the Federal Republic of Germany, if a traveller or representative terminates his contract without notice on grounds of serious mis-conduct by the employer, he has the option to allow himself to be bound or to refuse;   if he does not give notice of refusal within one month of termination, the clause stands.   In Argentina, Luxembourg and the Netherlands the clause is not operative if the employer terminates the contract without due notice or if for any reason the dismissal is wrongful;   a similar position has been taken by certain courts in France.[1]

It is clearly in the interest of the traveller himself to avoid as far as possible such restrictions on finding new employ-ment after termination.   However, the weakness of his bargaining position may force him to accept the employer's terms if he wants the job.[2]

Moreover, once the employment relationship has begun, his fear of the consequences of implementation of the radius clause may keep him in the job when for some reason he would prefer to seek employ-ment elsewhere.

Once an employment contract comprising a radius clause has been signed by the parties, it remains valid until the parties agree to modify it or until it is overturned or modified by a court of law.   It is understandable that a traveller seeking to remain in his employer's good books may be hesitant to seek to have the clause modified - if necessary by legal process - as long as his contract lasts.   Thus, when the contract is terminated the initial position of weakness is likely to remain.

Legal positions regarding radius clauses

Legislators have sought, in a variety of ways, to reconcile the two issues of principle involved: the right of the entrepreneur to enjoy protection against a violation of his legitimate trade secrets; and the right of a worker, in accordance with the prin-ciple of freedom of employment, to seek employment where he wishes and to make use in one job of knowledge and experience acquired in previous jobs.

The general tendency appears to be to accept, explicitly or tacitly, the principle of the radius clause, while restricting its application in various ways.   In addition, in considering the degree of applicability of the various restrictions - and in coun-tries in which the law does not give guidance on the subject, such as England and Wales and France - the courts have tended to examine in detail not only the intentions of the parties, but the practical consequences of the application of the clause, thus

---

[1] See André Brun and Henri Galland: Droit du travail (2nd edition, Paris, Sirey, 1978), Vol. 1, pp. 499 ff.

[2] See p. 38.

supplementing the provisions of the law by considerations of fairness. Thus in many cases, where the consequences of the application of the clause appear excessive in view of the facts, radius clause agreements have been modified or overturned by the courts.

The attitudes of the different legal systems - as laid down by statute or established in case law - vary.

In England and Wales, where no specific legislation on the subject exists, a radius clause agreement is liable to be deemed prima facie to be in restraint of trade and thus void as a matter of public policy. It will be upheld by the courts only if (a) it is no wider than is reasonably necessary for the protection of the person in favour of whom it is imposed; (b) it is also reasonable with reference to the person making the promise and to the public interest; and (c) there is valuable consideration for the promise. The interpretation of these principles tends to be restrictive; in the case of commercial travellers the clause will only be enforceable to safeguard the employer from injury by misuse of the employee's acquaintance with customers, i.e. from unfair competition rather than from competition per se.[1] Each case is dealt with on its individual merits; thus a radius clause may be upheld even though unlimited in geographical coverage or valid for the whole life of the traveller if the circumstances justify this.

In other countries of Western Europe, the applicable statutes and case law reflect a less extreme position. While recognising the legitimacy of clauses restraining generally the use in the service of one employer of knowledge and secrets acquired with a previous employer, they nevertheless tend to limit their application on the basis of considerations of necessity and equity and to set restrictions of a general character which, if exceeded, make the relevant provision, or the entire agreement, void or unenforceable.[2] The legal provisions applied are normally those applicable to employees in general, adapted in their application to the peculiar circumstances of commercial travellers.[3]

---

[1] Stephens: Commentaries of the Laws of England (London, Butterworth, 1950), pp. 55 ff.

[2] In France special rules governing radius clause agreements applicable to commercial travellers and representatives are laid down in the national interoccupational agreement for travellers, representatives and local agents dated 3 October 1975.

[3] In the Federal Republic of Germany the reverse took place; in 1970 the Federal Labour Court declared the rules governing radius clauses applicable to commercial employees applicable to non-commercial employees as well. See Entscheidungen des Bundesarbeitsgerichts (Berlin, New York, Walter de Gruyter), Vol. 22, 1972, p. 324.

The following general rules are found in the legislation of a number of countries:

(a) The radius clause must be in writing, on pain of invalidity.

(b) The signatory must enjoy legal capacity at the time of signature of the contract; in other words, a radius clause agreement signed by a person who is a minor at the time of signature is not valid, even if he subsequently becomes of age during the period of validity of the contract.

(c) The radius clause is invalid if termination occurs during probation or during the early months of employment; a traveller is unlikely to have become a potentially dangerous competitor in such a short time.

(d) Unless the traveller is earning more than a set minimum amount at the time of termination, the radius clause will not be valid (the minimum is usually set so low that a traveller earning less is unlikely to cause serious prejudice to the employer's interests when working in competition with him).

(e) The clause must seek to protect a legitimate business interest of the employer and may be declared unenforceable to the extent that it goes beyond that aim.   Thus, its validity is usually confined to the geographical area and the lines of goods in which competitive activity by the traveller could cause real prejudice to the employer - in practical terms, this means the area in which the traveller was working, and the lines of goods he was handling, at the time of termination. It could not, however, be invoked to prevent a traveller from working for a competitor in the same area but in a non-selling capacity.[1]   In Switzerland the validity of the clause lapses where it can be established that the employer has no real interest in the continuation of the restraint (e.g. where he has ceased manufacture of the type of goods covered).

(f) The scope of the clause must not be such as to place unreasonable obstacles in the way of the future career development of the traveller, taking all circumstances into account.   Thus an agreement which, for example, had the effect of preventing a traveller from earning a livelihood in his chosen profession, or forced him to move to another country to exercise it, could be held invalid.

---

[1] Similarly, a conditional radius clause (i.e. one which the employer can invoke or not according to whether or not he considers a new job found by his former employee to be competitive or not) has been declared unenforceable in the Federal Republic of Germany, since it hinders the employee in the search for a new job and at the same time offers the employer a means of avoiding payment of compensation (Entscheidungen des Bundesarbeitsgerichts, Vol. 22, loc. cit., pp. 324-325).

(g) A maximum period of validity must be set. In the Federal
Republic of Germany it is two years; in Austria and Belgium
it is one year; in Italy and Switzerland it is three years;
in Denmark it is one year unless compensation for the
curtailment of earning power is paid.

(h) In consideration of compliance with the clause, financial
compensation is payable. (This is in fact the only positive
obligation of the employer.) The minimum amount set in
Belgium[1] and the Federal Republic of Germany is half of the
traveller's earnings at the time of termination for every
year of restraint; in Austria the full amount of lost
earnings is payable; in France it is two-thirds of earnings
(less expenses) during the last 12 months preceding termination if the period of restraint exceeds one year, and one-
third if it is less. In the Netherlands the amount may be
set by the courts on the basis of equity. The general
practice appears to be to pay the compensation in monthly
instalments throughout the period of restraint. In
Switzerland the relevant section of the Code of Obligations
lays down no obligation to pay compensation, but it appears
that in many cases employers pay a former employee full salary
during the period of restraint. Failure to make provision
for compensation of any kind, or the setting of compensation
at a level less than the minimum stipulated by law, may in
certain cases make a radius clause agreement null and void
or unenforceable by the employer.[2] In the Netherlands the
law leaves the fixing of the amount of compensation payable
to the courts.

The compensation is not payable, or not payable in full, in
all cases. Thus, in the Federal Republic of Germany the amount
may be reduced if, taken together with any earnings he may be
receiving from employment not covered by the radius clause, it
brings his total income up to an amount significantly in excess of
his final earnings with the previous employer. In France, if
termination is due to resignation by the traveller, the amount of
the compensation payable is reduced by half. In Italy no
compensation is payable, and in Denmark compensation is payable
only if the period of restraint exceeds one year.

In some countries the employer may waive the application of
the radius clause before termination of the contract; if he does
so, his liability to pay compensation lapses at the end of a
stipulated period following the waiver.

Extent of the safeguards provided

The protection offered to the commercial traveller or representative by the law with regard to radius clause agreements thus
lays down certain requirements of form or substance, failure to
comply with which may make the agreement as a whole, or certain

---

[1] In addition, in Belgium the existence of a radius clause
creates a presumption of entitlement to a goodwill indemnity.

[2] See, for instance, in the Federal Republic of Germany: Ents-
cheidungendes Bundesarbeitsgerichts, Vol. 22, loc. cit., p. 125.

provisions of it, either null and void (i.e. may not be invoked by either party) or unforceable (in which case the employer cannot demand the enforcement of the agreement as it stands, but the traveller has the choice of refusing to be bound or of accepting the restraint provided that the offending clauses are appropriately modified).   The legislation of some countries is in fact so framed as to render substantial numbers of radius clauses illicit or of such a nature as to call for modification by the courts.[1] However, in view of the importance of case law in determining the legal position in a particular case, the changes which are con- tinually taking place in the attitudes of the courts on specific points, and the time which it may take to dispose of a case - up to seven years in a difficult and contested one - a traveller to whom a radius clause applies and who leaves his employment may find himself for a considerable period in a position of legal uncertainty and personal insecurity as regards the licitness of taking up a new job.

This insecurity is heightened by the effect, or potential effect, of the contractual penalty clauses contained in a number of agreements.   These clauses provide that, where a traveller or representative commits a breach of the radius clause, he must pay an agreed penalty to the former employer, without any requirement on the part of the latter to prove actual prejudice arising from the breach.   Such a stipulation may in some countries be included in the contract without prejudice to the employer's right to seek compensation for actual prejudice caused by the breach.   The amount of the penalty may be considerable;   but the courts may reduce it if they consider it excessive.

In addition, limits are sometimes set on the amounts of penalties;   thus in France, under the collective agreement for travellers and representatives, the penalty may not exceed his earnings from his former employer during the last 24 months of his employment.   In Belgium the law sets the maximum at three months' earnings, but the employer can claim more on proof of actual prejudice suffered.   In Italy, penalty clauses do not appear to exist;   if the former employee breaches the clause, the damages payable will be based on actual prejudice proved by the employer.

Even where safeguards of this kind exist, the situation of a traveller or representative under a penalty clause is fraught with uncertainty.   This will be particularly the case where there is doubt over whether the penalty, once paid, releases the traveller from further obligations under the radius clause (as is the case in Austria) or whether the full penalty may be exacted in respect of every act committed in breach of the clause - for instance, in the case of a commercial traveller, every order taken on behalf of a

---

[1] In Switzerland, for instance, the law provides that a radius clause is not valid unless the employment relationship has given the traveller a knowledge of the clientele;   that that knowledge can be put to use;   and that its use is liable to cause the employer significant prejudice (Schweingruber, op. cit., p. 230).

competitor.[1] Moreover, over and above the amount of the penalty,
the former employer may seek damages for actual prejudice suffered.
Lastly, in some countries he is entitled to apply to the courts for
an order requiring his former employee to cease and desist from
alleged breaches of a radius clause - for instance, in the case of
a traveller, from working for a firm which the former employer
alleges to be a competitor - and return any compensation previously
paid.[2] Even where the traveller is convinced that his case is a
sound one, uncertainty over the outcome of the proceedings will
place him under considerable strain.

The employer of a commercial traveller or representative has
an arsenal of legal weapons at his disposal to prevent what he
judges to be non-compliance with a radius clause. The traveller,
for his part, is in an extremely vulnerable position. He may feel
unable to take up a new job because to do so might render him liable
to payment of an unforeseeable amount of damages to his former
employer - or, if he takes it, he does so in the perpetual fear
that he may be obliged to give it up. Moreover, legal proceedings
may go on for years after the end of the period of restraint. Even
if he wins his case in the end, he will have suffered anxiety over
the whole period of the proceedings, his career progress may have
been seriously impeded, and he may have suffered financial
prejudice as well.

*

*   *

The radius clause and its enforcement as relating to commercial travellers and representatives has given rise to considerable
controversy in recent years. From the employers' side, it is
argued that a traveller's replacement cannot hope to take over his
predecessor's job fully unless the latter refrains from all competing activity in the sector concerned, and that the transfer of the
clientele implies of itself an obligation not to compete, especially
where a goodwill indemnity has been paid. On the travellers' side,
it is asserted that the principle of freedom of employment requires
that the obligations of a traveller to his employer should cease
on termination of the contract of employment and that the only
competition to be expressly prohibited is that falling under the
legislation on unfair competition.[3] However, among the unions

---

[1] This extreme view was taken in a ruling of the French Cour de
Cassation dated 20 February 1975, reported in Recueil Dalloz-Sirey,
1976, Jurisprudence, p. 142, with a note by Y. Serra.

[2] Grüll: Die Konkurrenzklausel (Heidelberg, Verlagsgesellschaft
Recht und Wirtschaft), pp. 58-59; Y. Serra: L'obligation de non
concurrence (Paris, Sirey, 1970), pp. 194 ff.

[3] It has also been suggested that penalty clauses are
inequitable, on the grounds, first, that the weaker party to the
agreement would reject them if he were in a position to do so, and
secondly, that they enable the stronger party to determine the
penalties applicable without reference to the law or the machinery
of justice. See the note by Y. Serra on the case mentioned in the
note above.

themselves opinion appears to be divided, some being for the abolition of the radius clause, others being prepared to accept the principle with safeguards; the latter seems to be the approach to have evolved in the consultations within the European Economic Community in the proposed directive on equality of treatment for commercial representatives.

While the radius clause may provide legal certainty as regards the right to prospect that part of the employer's clientele which was previously prospected by the departed traveller,[1] its application in practice can give rise to serious problems of personal and financial insecurity for the traveller concerned and in particular gravely circumscribe his ability to find new employment or to change jobs, depending upon the degree of rigour with which the individual employer enforces the clause and his intention in including it in the contract.[2] The fact that radius clause disputes occur frequently, notwithstanding the reluctance which travellers must feel to enter into such a commitment, suggests that acceptance of the clause is to some extent imposed; and all the safeguards provided by the law do not protect the traveller fully from insecurity and possible harassment to which his initial lack of bargaining power leaves him exposed.

Paradoxically, a traveller or representative who is particularly good at his job appears to be especially liable to have the radius clause invoked against him on account of the potential threat he may constitute to his employer if he enters the service of a competitor, and is thus most liable to have his personal career development hindered as a consequence.

Under the current legislation, and unless commercial travellers and representatives can find more effective ways of resisting the inclusion of radius clauses in their contracts of employment - or, alternatively, unless the basis of adherence to the clause can be shifted from one of penalties for non-compliance to one of positive incentives to compliance (as opposed to compensation) - the present situation seems likely to continue.

---

[1] Y. Serra: La clause de non-concurrence, op. cit., p. 201.

[2] It has been suggested that employers sometimes insert radius clauses in their employees' contracts as a means of discouraging them from leaving (Schweingruber, op. cit., p. 239).

CHAPTER IX

PROBLEMS OF SPECIAL CATEGORIES
OF EXTERNAL SALESMEN

Older salesmen

A Swiss journalist, writing of the profession of commercial traveller, recently wrote:

A salesman has no right to grow old. He must always appear fresh and full of life and energy to his customers. As competition stiffens, he cannot count in his declining years on his customers remaining faithful; he must all the time be breaking new ground and defending what he has already gained.[1]

While this statement is probably an over-simplification, it nevertheless reflects a measure of reality.

Although it is impossible to generalise on the subject, it has nevertheless been observed in a number of countries that a salesman's performance as measured in terms of business gained is frequently affected by age. Up to a point, it improves as he gains in skills and experience; but as he reaches and passes the peak of his powers in middle age it often tends to level off or even begins to decline slowly.[2]

Where this situation arises, it is likely to create strains for the traveller.

From the purely financial standpoint, the degree of strain will vary according to his conditions of employment. A traveller on straight salary, or with a relatively small element of commission in his remuneration, may be unaffected; if his conditions of employment provide for some form of seniority-based increment, his pay may actually continue to rise. However, for a traveller who is paid mainly or entirely by commission, a fall in turnover will have an immediate impact on earnings, on termination benefit entitlement, and possibly on pension entitlements as well.

A more general potential source of stress is to be found in his relations with his employer or his sales manager. Any decline in performance will be immediately visible in the form of a decline in sales. The fear that such a decline will attract the employer's attention and draw comment, advice, criticism, and possibly the threat of dismissal can be a source of considerable anxiety to a traveller who fears he is passing his peak of effectiveness; and as he grows older this anxiety may affect his attitude towards his work and his behaviour generally. Such a situation can create problems for his employer too; however well-disposed the latter may be, he cannot afford to see the volume of his sales decline.

---

[1] Le Mercure, 14 March 1978.

[2] Smyth and Murphy (op. cit., p. 35) suggest that the peak of performance is reached as early as in the late 30s.

On the other hand, "there are many salesmen working today, and doing their jobs well, who are far beyond the age at which office and other workers are retired or pensioned".[1]

A third factor, which eventually affects all travellers and representatives who for one reason or another are not considered for managerial positions, is that of coming to terms with the realisation that "this is as far as I shall get", either in general or in the jobs they occupy. The realisation of this position is liable to give rise to feelings of insecurity, frustration and disillusionment, especially in a society which identifies prestige with advancement to the ranks of management.

The reaction of the traveller or representative who feels that he has been passed by in this way will vary. One may move to another job where he believes that the opportunities for winning recognition may be greater. Another may decide to rest on his laurels, relax his efforts to create new business and concentrate on holding existing customers. A third may decide to start his own business.

The attitudes of employers on the problem of ageing varies. Some appear to prefer younger travellers, on the grounds that they are more alert and more receptive to new methods of selling and merchandising. Others consider that an experienced traveller is a valuable asset to a firm; as one writer[2] has put it:

Because of their years of experience, wealth of knowledge, and long friendships with many buyers, [older salesmen] can often out-produce the younger salesmen. In many cases, older salesmen get on with older clients much better than younger salesmen do because the older men have a common outlook on life and on business problems.

In many cases, it may be possible to sustain the capacities of older salesmen by training them in new selling techniques and new behaviour patterns. As the same writer says:[3] " ... these experienced salesmen can learn when they are properly motivated and given sufficient time, training and encouragement".

There is also a growing recognition in some management circles that the loss or demotivation of older salesmen is a matter requiring positive action.

A symposium on the motivation of older salesmen[4] has proposed a number of possible forms of remedial action.

The first of these relates to the attitude of management towards the profession. It suggests that preparation for the "moment of truth" should begin on the very day that a man is interviewed, among other things, by building up the image of selling as

[1] J.C. Apsley (ed.): The sales manager's handbook, seventh edition (Chicago and London, Dartnell Corporation, 1956), p. 588.

[2] Stroh, op. cit., p. 235.

[3] ibid., p. 235.

[4] Motivating the older salesman: a symposium, Experiences in Marketing Management, No. 5 (New York, National Industrial Conference Board, 1964).

a career and emphasising its importance to the survival of the
company and the opportunities for self-fulfilment that it offers;
and, as a corollary, being more open about opportunities to rise
to management level, especially where the prospective employer is
sure the newcomer will not qualify.

Secondly, sales managers should be taught the best methods of
handling older and possibly more knowledgeable salesmen who are
placed under their leadership.

Thirdly, every effort should be made to raise the older salesmen'a self-esteem by giving open recognition of his achievements in
various ways.

Fourthly, appropriate retraining, designed not only to bring
the older salesman up to date on product development and selling
techniques and aids but also to rejuvenate his thinking and help
him develop new approaches, should be made available.

Lastly, the jobs of older salesmen should where possible be
redesigned to give them scope for exercising their accumulated
talents and experience more fully and developing their careers
further, for instance by creating posts of specialist or senior
salesmen to service key accounts, supervisory or consultant posts
without managerial responsibilities, or assigning older salesmen
to task forces to undertake specially difficult assignments of a
temporary character.

An alternative possibility is to transfer an older salesman
whose performance is flagging to less exacting work in the employing firm's offices.   This may give rise to a reduction in earnings
and, where retirement benefits are calculated on the basis of
earnings during the years immediately preceding retirement, in termination benefits and pension entitlements as well; but this effect
will be lessened to the extent that the pension is calculated on
the basis of average earnings over the employee's whole lifetime or
during the best years of his career, as is the case in a number of
countries.

It should also be mentioned that, where provisions safeguarding
the jobs of older workers in general or providing special assistance
for them in the event of unemployment exist in laws or collective
agreements, commercial travellers and representatives with employee
status may also take advantage of those provisions.

Salesmen soliciting orders
from private individuals

Certain categories of persons directly soliciting the custom
of private individuals also seek orders for goods and services on
behalf of and for the account of employers or principals, and may
thus be distinguished from itinerant vendors and hawkers, who make
physical sales.

In some countries the obtaining of orders for goods from private individuals in their homes accounts for a considerable proportion of the total sales of certain sectors of industry.   Thus in
France in 1970, 50 per cent of all sales of sewing machines and

30 per cent of sales of electrical household appliances were made in this way.[1]

The view is widely held that door-to-door salesmen should not be included[2] within the category of commercial travellers and representatives. The principal consideration advanced in support of this attitude is that the great majority of them are concerned not with the building up of a clientele of regular customers, but with one-time sales, and that the balance between making a sale and satisfying the customer is therefore liable to be tipped in favour of the former factor. They are frequently shunned by commercial travellers and representatives serving "the trade", who consider that they do not always respect normal standards of probity and thus bring the entire profession of external selling into disrepute. However, many of them represent extremely reputable firms manufacturing goods of high quality and offering all necessary guarantees of after-sales service. In addition, there is evidence that in some cases this method of sale is appreciated by customers - for instance, where demonstration and explanation is needed or, as in the case of certain toiletries, housewives of modest means are reluctant to go to a perfumery for fear of being looked down on by the sales staff.[3]

In a number of countries home sales are subject to special legislation designed to protect the consumer; thus, in Austria they are forbidden to offer certain types of goods[4] for sale, and are subject to restrictions as regards sales of other goods (e.g., the customer must complete the order form in his own handwriting and send it to the firm by post). They are also subject to registration requirements. In some countries, too, the principal manufacturers of goods sold in this way have formed associations to establish standards of selling ethics.

In Japan , where door-to-door selling has expanded rapidly in recent years in a number of sectors of the domestic market (in particular those in which manufacturers have not yet established networks of wholesale and retail outlets), the Government has sought not only to check abuses but also to improve ethical and professional standards within this group of workers and also to improve their conditions of employment; legislation on the subject was adopted in 1976. Subsequently, in implementation of administrative guidelines issued by the competent ministry, some 50 companies and 12 sectoral associations established in March 1979 a Door-to-Door Sales Enterprise Council to promote, on a voluntary basis, improvements in the training and briefing of door-to-door salesmen and to

---

[1] Marketing: La vente (Paris, SEMA, 1972), pp. 179-186.

[2] This was the view taken by the compilers of ISCO, which places them in a separate unit group (452: Street vendors, canvassers and newsvendors) under the occupational title of "canvassers".

[3] Cases quoted in Marketing: La vente, op. cit.

[4] The principal of these are food, toilet articles, toxic substances, pharmaceutical preparations, textiles, jewellery, gold and silverware, weapons and ammunition, fireworks and tombstones (Industries Order, section 57).

deal with consumers' complaints.   In France, the manufacturers of
a number of lines of goods, a considerable proportion of which are
sold to private individuals in this way, have formed an association
for the training of their sales forces and the maintenance of
adequate standards of ethics in this branch of selling.

While some direct salesmen have employee status, the majority
appear to be engaged on a commission-only basis, paying all their
own expenses, working in accordance with their employer's instructions but enjoying none of the protections which accompany employee
status and being extremely dependent on the goodwill of the
employer for job security - and even, it seems, for their pay in
certain cases.   In Japan, in the cosmetics sector, door-to-door
salesmen are even expected by some companies to buy from the company
the samples they use in their work and also small items to offer as
gifts to prospective customers.

It was precisely to protect persons seeking orders directly
from private individuals from abuses in this regard that in
Argentina the legislation on commercial travellers was amended
during its discussion by the legislative assembly to give such persons employee status on an equal footing with commercial travellers
and representatives provided they met the conditions laid down in
the Act.   In Brazil and Panama, they are also entitled to employee
status under the same conditions, subject to the proviso that they
do not work for more than one employer.   In Italy the situation
under the national collective agreement is similar.   In New
Zealand door-to-door salesmen are considered as falling within the
scope of the definition of commercial travellers.   In Switzerland,
the legislation applicable to commercial travellers also applies
to external salesmen visiting private customers;   it also allows
them, unlike travellers in general, to enter into del credere
agreements (in view of the particular nature of the clientele) provided that a reasonable additional commission is paid.   In the
different states of Australia, their conditions of employment are
regulated by separate awards.

The granting of employee status to persons in this category,
while not solving all their problems by any means, has nevertheless
provided them with a much-needed minimum level of protection in the
countries concerned.

Travellers and representatives employed by firms situated in countries other than those in which they work

With the expansion of international trade, firms are employing
external sales personnel in foreign countries.   Their situation
gives rise to a number of problems which may be extremely complex.

A firm wishing to develop its business in a foreign country
may send a traveller on repeated visits, maintaining his base in the
country of the employing firm;   it may send a traveller to take up
residence in the foreign country;   or it may appoint a traveller or
representative already resident in the country concerned (often a
citizen of that country).

One of the first problems to arise will be the choice of the legislation to govern the contract of employment and of the courts competent to settle disputes. In the first of the cases mentioned, the legislation and courts of the home country are most likely to be selected; but in the other two cases the issue may be complicated by mandatory provisions of the legislation of the host country.

Problems may also arise in connection with the right to work. A traveller visiting a foreign country temporarily may be allowed to exercise his profession under bilateral trade agreements; but a traveller wishing to reside in a foreign country will be subject to the legislation governing the employment of aliens.

Taxation may also give rise to problems; in some cases a traveller abroad may be subject to double taxation, in others he may escape taxation altogether.

Social protection is a problem of special importance. A traveller residing in a foreign country is likely to be required to pay contributions (sometimes his employers' contributions as well as his own) to a national social security scheme; at the same time, it may be in his interests to keep up his membership of the scheme or schemes in his own country. On his return to his home country, as mentioned earlier, the problem of transfer of accumulated pension rights may arise. For a traveller working abroad from a base in his home country there is the problem of securing adequate care in the event of incapacity for work incurred in the foreign country, especially where no reciprocity arrangements on the social security questions exist between the two countries concerned. If he is a national of the country in which he is working, problems will arise if his employer refuses to register him with that country's national social insurance scheme; in particular, if he becomes incapacitated for work involving travel, he is unlikely to be able to fall back on a sedentary job in his employer's head office and may not only find it difficult to obtain new employment but also be ineligible for unemployment assistance.

Other problems which may arise relate to such subjects as difficulties in negotiating with customers on the legislation to govern the transaction; responsibility for the successful outcome of transactions; and differences between national legislations applicable to the conditions of employment of commercial travellers.

While considerations of space preclude more than a brief survey of the kinds of problems which a traveller working for a firm in another country may have to face, mention should be made of one particularly interesting attempt to deal with at least some of them on a multilateral basis.

The European Economic Community is seeking to overcome the problem of anomalies of applicable legislation, as far as its member States are concerned, by the introduction of a proposal for a directive[1] designed to harmonise the legislation of its Members on the subject of commercial travellers and representatives. The

---

[1] This draft directive follows on a similar proposal, relating to commercial agents, which at the time of writing (August 1979) had passed through most of the procedures required for final adoption.

directive seeks, first of all, to eliminate certain legal
disparities affecting conditions of competition and the exercise
of the profession.   For instance, at present, goodwill indemnities
are payable in some countries but not in others;   since the cost of
a traveller will be higher in a country where they are payable than
in one where they are not, an employer who is not required to pay
the indemnity will enjoy a competitive advantage.   Secondly, it
seeks to provide a minimum level of protection for commercial travellers and representatives vis-à-vis their employers (to compensate
to some extent for their inferior bargaining power), without prejudice to any more favourable conditions which they may enjoy under
national legislation.   Negotiations on the proposal appear to have
reached an advanced stage;   and travellers' organisations in some
non-member countries - Spain and Sweden - have adopted it as a
basis for negotiations with employers' organisations on conditions
of employment.

This proposal does not cover all the problems of the commercial
traveller working for a firm in another country;   in particular, it
deals with questions of social protection only in the most general
of terms.   However, it has considerable interest as an attempt,
within a group of countries, not only to provide a uniform solution
to some of the problems affecting travellers and representatives
employed by firms in countries other than those in which they work,
but also to provide minimum standards in respect of certain conditions of employment peculiar to the profession.

CONCLUSIONS

In the resolution on the legal position of commercial and industrial travellers and representatives which it adopted at its 1935 Session, the Advisory Committee on Salaried Employees expressed the wish that "in every country regulations should be issued to define the legal status of travellers and representatives, which, while taking into account their special conditions of employment, should place them under the legislation for the social protection, insurance and welfare of salaried employees". It went on to propose a minimum list of subjects to be covered by these regulations - written contracts, notice of termination, freedom from liability in the event of insolvency of the buyer and the right to goodwill indemnities.

Since then a number of countries have adopted legislation conferring employee status (and thus entitlement to the protection of labour and social legislation) on various categories of persons habitually and regularly working outside the premises of the firms they represent, visiting customers with a view to obtaining orders for the goods or services offered by those firms, provided that they comply with certain conditions and in particular that they make no transactions for their own account. Evidence also exists of a tendency, in some of these countries, for the legislature or the courts to take into account the relative weakness of the contractual position of travellers and representatives (inevitable in a branch of activity in which individual contracts are the rule rather than the exception) by laying the burden of proof of non-employee status on the employer or by discounting certain factors which might otherwise be considered as evidence of non-employee status. Courts of law have in some cases played an important part in clarifying certain aspects of the legislation adopted.

Experience with the application of this legislation has brought out a certain number of useful guidelines regarding the conditions to be observed in conferment of employee status on persons in this occupational group. It has also revealed a number of possible shortcomings and loopholes and ways of dealing with them.

A number of countries have taken no specific action since the 1935 meeting, but there is evidence that in some of them travellers and representatives do enjoy employee status, either under previously existing legislation on the profession or by extension to them of the protection provided by labour and social legislation (e.g., social insurance legislation) to workers or salaried employees in general (or, in some cases, in the private sector).

Where specific regulations exist, they frequently apply not only to salesmen working for one employer but also to those working for several employers or paid on commission only - although in several countries a traveller working for more than one principal simultaneously is not entitled to employee status.

In the majority of countries the parties enjoy considerable freedom under the law regarding the form of contracts of employment; written contracts for commercial travellers and representatives are compulsory in only a few. However, in a number of the countries in which the requirement does not exist, guidelines have been formulated in statute and case law for determining whether a particular contract, whatever its form and content, does in fact confer employee status on the salesman concerned.

As regards termination, the attainment of employee status has given the travellers and representatives concerned the same entitlements as most other employees in the same country; in a few cases they enjoy more favourable terms under the law and collective agreements.

Freedom from liability in the event of non-performance by the buyer seems to have been substantially achieved in the countries covered by the inquiry. Formal del credere arrangements are subject to restriction, or even forbidden by law, in certain countries; in most cases the traveller merely loses entitlement to commission on a transaction in which the buyer does not perform. In several countries, however, once the employer has accepted an order, the right of the traveller to commission on that order stands, irrespective of the outcome of the transaction.

The situation has not changed greatly regarding the right of a traveller or representative to special compensation in respect of his personal contribution to the growth of the clientele. While commercial agents are generally considered under commercial law to build up a clientele of their own and to make it over to their principals on termination, the same considerations are not always deemed to apply to employee travellers and representatives, who are considered to be building up the clientele of their employers. In a few countries, however, the principle of financial recognition, on a traveller's departure, of his contribution to the development of his employer's clientele is recognised either by the law or in collective agreements.

Finally, the extent to which the conditions of employment of travellers and representatives are determined by collective agreement varies considerably from country to country. In a few countries there are national intersectoral agreements specifically for them (although these do not always contain specific rules governing all aspects of the employment relationship); in other countries they may be covered by collective agreements for specific industrial sectors; in others the majority are engaged under individual contracts of employment. In countries in which the level of unionisation among travellers and representatives is low, this situation seems likely to continue.

In addition to the problems mentioned by the Advisory Committee, certain other problems have emerged following the attainment of employee status by large numbers of travellers and representatives. The following are some of them.

First, mention should be made of the disputes which frequently arise in some countries over whether a traveller's contract is in fact a contract of employment, which frequently have to be referred to courts of law. Where the legal proceedings are not expeditiously terminated, the traveller may for a protracted period live and work in a state of insecurity (he may, for instance, not be able to join the social security scheme for employed persons until the question is settled).

A second set of problems arises from the frequent absence of standards regarding the content of contracts. In the absence of guidelines on the subjects to be covered, contracts may be drafted in a manner which leaves the intentions of the parties unclear, and may also leave the traveller in a position of weakness vis-à-vis his employer on specific questions.

Thirdly, travellers and representatives paid wholly or substantially by commission still share to some degree the entrepreneurial risks of their employers. When business is slow, they may find their incomes reduced owing to circumstances outside their control, and where payment of commission depends on successful completion of the transaction, they may lose commission through no fault of their own. In addition, problems sometimes arise regarding methods of ensuring a regular minimum level of income for travellers and representatives whose earnings consist substantially or entirely of commission.

Payment of expenses, too, can give rise to problems. This is especially the case where commission is deemed to include expenses, since the loss of a commission automatically entails loss of expense payments, although the expenses have actually been incurred; in addition, expense allowances of this kind may prove inadequate where a special effort is demanded of a traveller. The application of the general principle that an employer should reimburse the business expenses of his employees appears to be imperfect in such cases.

Hours of work and weekly rest, although apparently less of a problem than in the past, nevertheless remain problem areas.

As regards social security, there are cases in which the arrangements for sick pay cover only part of the earnings lost by the traveller.

As regards termination, the conferring of employee status has given rise to controversy over the validity of the principle of the radius clause, and of the penalty clauses frequently appended, in application to travellers and representatives with employee status.

Commercial travellers and representatives employed by firms in other countries have their own special problems.

Lastly, it may be wondered whether the extension of employee status, and of the requirements of labour legislation, to persons making direct sales to private individuals would not be conducive to an improvement in the condition of workers in this category and of the image of the entire group.

Solutions to these different problems will doubtless be worked out in due course by discussion among the parties concerned. It is hoped that the material contained in this study will be of assistance to those parties in their search for solutions.